The Young People's History of America's Wars Series

By DON LAWSON

The Colonial Wars

The American Revolution

The War of 1812

The United States in the Mexican War

The United States in the Civil War

The United States in the Indian Wars

The United States in the Spanish-American War

The United States in World War I

The United States in World War II

The United States in the Korean War

The United States in the Vietnam War

The United States in the Vietnam War

Don Lawson

Thomas Y. Crowell   New York

Designed by Al Cetta

Library of Congress Cataloging in Publication Data
Lawson, Don.
The United States in the Vietnam War.

(The Young people's history of America's wars)
SUMMARY: Explains the political, social, economic,
and military aspects of the Vietnam War, the longest
in American history.
1. Vietnamese Conflict, 1961–1975—United States—
Juvenile literature. 2. United States—History—
1945–   —Juvenile literature. [1. Vietnamese Conflict,
1961–1975—United States. 2. United States—
History—1945–   ] I. Title.
DS558.L38 1981   959.704'33'73   80–2460
ISBN 0–690–04104–7
ISBN 0–690–04105–5

6   7   8   9   10
First Edition

To Tom Grey, who was there

Acknowledgments

I wish to thank the United States Defense Department, the Air Force, Army, Navy, and Marine Corps for furnishing me with a broad selection of photographs to use in this book. Particular thanks are due to William R. Drobnick, U.S. Army Magazine and Book Coordinator, for his aid in obtaining particular photographs and in answering specific questions regarding factual details. Any errors in fact or judgment, however, are my own.

I also wish to thank the family of the late Army Master Sergeant Bobbie Loeschner, Sr., and his son Bobbie, Jr., for their cooperation in supplying pictures and information about the "one good thing that came out of the Vietnam War." Before his untimely death, Sergeant Loeschner was most generous with his time and great knowledge about the grunts' role in Vietnam. Special thanks also go to Ethel Daccardo, who first told me the Loeschners' heartwarming story and cooperated in obtaining photographs.

Finally, my thanks once again to Bob McCullough for an excellent map.

Contents

1. The Battle of Dien Bien Phu   1
2. Geneva Peace Conference:
   Prelude to War   16
3. Incident in the Gulf of Tonkin:
   The War Begins   31
4. Unconventional Vietcong Warfare,
   Conventional U.S. Methods   49
5. "Winning the Hearts and Minds
   of the People"   62
6. Body Counts and Kill Ratios   73
7. The Tet Offensive   89
8. The My Lai Massacre   103
9. Vietnamization—and Defeat   111
10. Aftermath   125
    Further Reading   138
    Index   143

"Probably the only people who have ever had the historical sense of inevitable victory are the Americans."

—Sir Denis Brogan

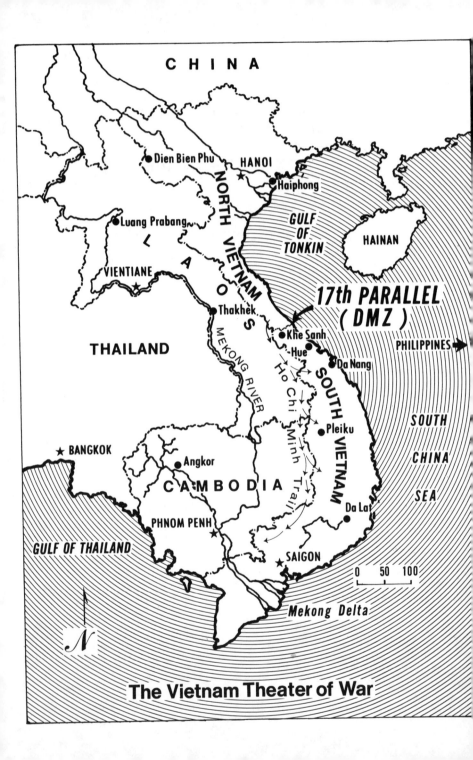

The Vietnam Theater of War

1.
THE BATTLE OF DIEN BIEN PHU

On an early spring day in 1954, General Paul Ely, chief of staff of the French army, flew from Paris to Washington, D.C. He was on an emergency mission. The purpose of General Ely's mission was to get the United States to enter the war that France was fighting against the Vietnamese Communists in Indochina.

In Washington General Ely met with top-ranking government officials, including United States President Dwight D. Eisenhower. General Ely told these officials that France wanted the United States to launch a massive air strike against the Communist military forces that had surrounded the French military forces at the village of Dien Bien Phu in North Vietnam. Unless the United States launched such an air strike, Ely insisted, France would be defeated at Dien Bien Phu and driven out of Indochina.

The United States had been seriously considering offering France just such air support for some time. The French had been fighting the Vietnamese Communists since 1946, and the United States had been supporting the French war effort with money, arms, and equipment.

This aid was given because many American leaders feared the loss of Indochina might lead to a complete take-over of the whole of Southeast Asia by the Communists. When it became clear that such short-of-war aid would not be enough to insure French victory, military intervention seemed the next logical step.

During his first few hours in Washington, French General Ely was encouraged to learn that a number of American leaders were in favor of entering the war as France's combat ally. He was told of a plan drawn up by the U.S. Joint Chiefs of Staff which called for an air strike against Communist Vietnamese supply bases near Dien Bien Phu. This strike was to be launched from aircraft carriers in the South China Sea near the Vietnam coast. In addition, American heavy bombers based in the Philippines would join in the strike.

If this first attack did not stop the Communist Vietnamese from overrunning Dien Bien Phu, then additional air strikes were to follow. (There was even some hint that the United States might use atomic bombs in the aerial bombardment.)* And if all else failed, American ground troops might be airlifted into Vietnam to fight side by side with the French.

But General Ely's emergency mission was doomed to failure.

Although he was a former Army general, Dwight Eisenhower had been elected Thirty-fourth president of the United States on a "peace" platform. Less than a decade before he took office to succeed Harry S Truman in 1953, Eisenhower had led the Allies to victory in

---

*Two aircraft carriers bearing nuclear weapons were, in fact, alerted to be sent to Indochina.

Europe in World War II. He had hoped the atom bombs dropped on Japan to end that war would mean an end to all warfare. But in 1950 when Truman still was president, North Korea, aided by the Soviet Union and Communist China, attacked South Korea. The United States and other members of the United Nations immediately went to war to defend the Republic of South Korea.

During Eisenhower's first year in office as president, he had successfully overseen a truce agreement signed in the Korean conflict. Eisenhower knew that the world in general, and the United States in particular, was war-weary. And from a professional soldier's viewpoint he shied away from getting bogged down in a major war on the vast landmass of Asia. He agreed with Army Chief of Staff Matthew B. Ridgway that such a war effort would be suicidal.

Eisenhower instructed his secretary of state, John Foster Dulles, to tell General Ely that the president could not authorize an air strike to save Dien Bien Phu without approval by the United States Congress. Congress, meanwhile, had indicated it would give no such approval.

General Ely was then faced with the sad duty of sending a telegram to General Henri Navarre, French commander in chief in Indochina, telling him that the beleaguered forces at Dien Bien Phu would have to fight on without further aid from the United States. And this, both Ely and Navarre knew, was also suicidal.

France had been a major colonial power in Indochina since the middle of the nineteenth century. This colonial empire was made up of the ancient kingdoms of Cambodia, Laos, and Vietnam. Japan took over this empire from France at the start of World War II. When the Japanese were driven out of the area at the end of World War II, France decided to return there and regain control of its rich rice fields and rubber plantations.

But the people of Indochina wanted to be independent. What was more important, they were willing to fight and die for "self-determination." They were led in this fight against the French by the *Vietminh,* or Vietnam Independence League.

The Vietminh was headed by a revolutionary leader named Ho Chi Minh and other Communist nationalists who were determined to destroy French colonialism and return ownership of the land to the people who farmed it and worked on it. Then profits from the crops would go directly to the people instead of being drained off by some foreign power.

In addition, Ho Chi Minh and his fellow revolutionaries were determined that the people of Indochina should govern themselves. In this way they were not unlike the French and American people who had fought and died for their independence in the French and the American revolutions in the eighteenth century.

Before the French could return to Indochina after World War II, Ho Chi Minh established a new government called the Democratic Republic of Vietnam (DRV) on September 2, 1945. Its headquarters were in North Vietnam. However, late in 1945 the French successfully regained possession of South Vietnam as well as Laos and Cambodia.

At first, neither the French nor the Vietminh seemed to want a war in Vietnam. In fact the French signed an agreement with Ho Chi Minh stating that the Democratic Republic of Vietnam was to be a free and independent state. In addition, it would have membership in a federation of Indochinese states, all of which would belong to the French Union. It was implied that the French Union would be similar to the British Commonwealth of Nations in that its members would be independent politically, but bound together economically. The French also agreed to let the South Vietnamese vote on whether or not they wanted to join politically with North Vietnam. Finally, the French agreed to withdraw all of their troops from Vietnam gradually.

Within a matter of months, however, it became clear that France had no intention of living up to any of its agreements. Soon both sides began to prepare for war. On November 23, 1946, the French sent airplanes and battleships to bomb the port of Haiphong, killing several thousand civilians. The Vietminh immediately struck back with guerrilla attacks throughout Vietnam. By mid-December full-scale warfare had begun.

During the first few months of the conflict it appeared that the French would defeat the Vietminh quickly and easily. The French military forces far outnumbered those of the Vietminh and almost at once took control of most of the major cities and main highways. But they were never able to control the rural villages and surrounding countryside. That would have demanded a vast supply of manpower that the French government was unwilling to commit to the struggle. And even so it is by no means sure that the Vietminh guerrillas could have been conquered.

The Vietminh forces were headed by a brilliant guerrilla leader named Vo Nguyen Giap. Giap, a former history teacher, was a great admirer of China's Mao Tse-tung whose Chinese Communists were in the final stages of driving Chiang Kai-shek's Nationalists out of China to the island of Formosa (today's Taiwan). Mao Tse-tung had perfected guerrilla warfare to a fine degree —he had even written a book on the subject—and Giap had memorized Mao's teachings.

One of Mao's guerrilla warfare maxims was that no military unit should confront the enemy unless the enemy was greatly outnumbered. Since the Vietminh were almost always outnumbered by the French, there were seldom any pitched battles. Instead, Giap's small bands of guerrillas lay in ambush along roads and trails, swiftly struck the advancing enemy, and then disappeared back into the jungle brush. They also moved by night, cutting off enemy supply and communications lines and disappearing before dawn. Often a French column approaching a village would find itself under sniper fire, but when the French took over the village the Vietminh snipers had once again retreated into the surrounding jungle. In retaliation against the villagers the French frequently took hostage or simply shot all of the able-bodied civilian men and boys.

The war dragged on in this murderously frustrating fashion for months and finally years. The French could not force the Vietminh into a series of major set piece battles and thus perhaps defeat them. And the Vietminh could not mount a large enough force or gather enough supplies and munitions to drive the French out of the country.

But in 1949 the picture began to change. The Chinese Communists finally completed their conquest of China and immediately began giving major military aid to the Vietminh. The political nature of the North Vietnamese government also began to change, as the Vietminh became more and more dependent on the Chinese not only for military aid but also for the training of troops in modern methods of warfare. Ho Chi Minh and his co-leaders had long been patriotic Vietnamese nationalists first and Communists second. Now they became Communists first and nationalists second, and patterned their government after the government of China and other Communist nations. The Vietnamese Communists, however, continued to act independently of China. They wanted no direct interference from *any* country in Vietnam's internal affairs.

It was at this point that the United States under President Truman began to give financial and war material aid to the French in Indochina. Then, when the United States entered the Korean War in June 1950, it meant that two major nations were fighting on the border of Communist China. Immediately, most of the nations that had fought in World War II began to fear another world war. Largely because of this fear, former general Eisenhower was elected to succeed Truman and when the Korean War ended the world breathed a bit easier.

But France was still bogged down in Indochina. During the Korean War, France and the United States had agreed that neither country would make peace with the Communists at the expense of the other. Consequently, the United States under Eisenhower continued to pour aid into the French Indochinese war effort even after a Korean truce had been signed. Nevertheless, actually left on their own to fight the war, the French decided to try to obtain a truce in Vietnam. By that time, however, Ho Chi Minh ignored all peace overtures. He was dedicated to full and complete independence for the Democratic Republic of Vietnam.

With a long series of combat successes and failures on both sides, the stalemated war dragged on into the early 1950s.

In 1953 General Henri Navarre was sent from Paris to take over as French commander in chief in Indochina. He had never been in Indochina, but he had been one of France's outstanding generals in Europe and Africa in World War II. Navarre thought he knew how to bring this war to a successful conclusion.

Navarre's plan was to build up the South Vietnamese military forces, or the Vietnamese National Army. These forces would be used to defend South Vietnam against the Vietminh. Then a major part of the French army would move into North Vietnam near Laos. There the French would be concentrated in a single, highly fortified camp. This, Navarre believed, would create an inviting target for the Vietminh to attack in force. Once the Vietminh had been lured into a major battle Navarre was certain the French could defeat them and take over complete control of North Vietnam.

In planning his traditional set piece battle Navarre made several major errors. First, he did not know that, aided by China, General Giap's guerrilla forces had now grown strong enough to fight successfully in a large single battle and not merely in scattered guerrilla actions. Second, Navarre thought the Vietminh could not move enough military arms, equipment, and supplies through the jungles and hills of North Vietnam to sustain a major attack on a fortified camp. In this Navarre was perhaps misled by the fact that his own supply situation could be taken care of by air drops from troop- and cargo-carrying American-made airplanes. The Vietminh, he knew, had no such air support available. What he did not know was that the Vietminh did have available an incredible amount of pack-carrying manpower that was matched only by an incredible amount of courage.

The place Navarre picked for his showdown with Giap's Vietminh forces was the village of Dien Bien Phu.* The village was situated ten miles from Laos in a valley some twelve miles long and about half that distance wide. Surrounding the valley were mountainous, jungle-covered hills. Dien Bien Phu formed the junction of three main roads. Navarre thought this road junction might further attract Giap since one of the roads led into Laos which the Vietminh had been threatening to invade.

Navarre's troops began parachuting into Dien Bien Phu late in 1953. Immediately they began fortifying the area and building an airstrip. More troops and supplies, arms, and equipment were then flown in until the French garrison numbered some 16,000 men. Included in the airborne equipment were dozens of artillery guns and a dozen tanks. The latter were flown in in pieces and reassembled at the camp. Navarre thought that the Vietminh would have no heavy artillery when they attacked, so the French artillery emplacements were not fortified or camouflaged. This was, perhaps, Navarre's third major mistake.

As the French buildup at Dien Bien Phu continued, Navarre received word from his intelligence sources that Giap planned on surrounding the fortified camp with some 50,000 Vietminh. Navarre, making a final error in judgment, refused to believe this information. There was

---

*Although it was not a large village, its name means Big (Dien) Frontier (Bien) Administration Center (Phu).

no way, Navarre insisted, that Giap could move that many men through hundreds of miles of jungle, let alone supply them once they had arrived.

What Navarre did not know was that in addition to 50,000 combat troops Giap had some 30,000 peasant porters who formed a river-like supply line leading through the jungle toward Dien Bien Phu. Usually these porters moved by night, but when they moved by day they actually tied together the treetops over their routes. Thus, as they moved through these tunnels of vegetation, they could not be seen by French aerial observers.

Giap's porters bore their loads on their backs or on pack animals or bicycles. The bicycles were not ridden but pushed and were specially reinforced so they could each haul as much as 500 pounds. In addition to food supplies, which consisted mainly of bags of rice, the porters carried thousands of rounds of ammunition for light infantry weapons as well as artillery shells. Somehow they were also able to manhandle heavy artillery guns along the crude jungle trails, and by year's end these guns were in place and carefully camouflaged in the hills surrounding the poorly fortified French camp.

General Navarre spent Christmas with his troops at Dien Bien Phu. He assured them that when the Vietminh attacked, the siege would last only a few days. Then he expected his forces to counterattack and destroy the enemy.

With those encouraging words Navarre flew back to Saigon in South Vietnam, leaving in immediate charge of the coming battle a tank officer, Colonel Christian de Castries, and a paratrooper, Lieutenant Colonel Pierre Langlais. Colonel Langlais had broken his leg when he first parachuted into Dien Bien Phu, but had insisted upon remaining on duty with his leg in a cast. He made his way about the camp on a pony supplied to him by Colonel de Castries. De Castries had had no experience in siege warfare, and Langlais's activities were extremely limited by his injury. Both, however, were courageous men and inspirational leaders.

De Castries and Langlais readied the French garrison for attack early in January. But no attack came. Wise in the ways of psychological warfare, General Giap knew that the French were now eager for battle and that a long, anxious delay would help destroy their morale. He was also wise in the ways of Vietnamese weather. He knew that in another month or two rain and fog would descend upon the valley. This would not hamper the movements of the Vietminh, but it would prevent French planes from flying in with troops and supplies or from flying out with the garrison's wounded. In addition, bad weather would prevent French flyers from attacking the Vietminh artillery positions once the Vietminh batteries opened fire and disclosed their locations.

Giap delayed his attack until March. Then, suddenly, on the evening of March 13, 1954, every heavy gun in the Vietminh arsenal opened fire on the Dien Bien Phu garrison. In a matter of moments the French camp was a shambles. Many of the unprotected French guns were promptly put out of action. The airstrip was pocked with shell holes. Telephone communication lines were cut, isolating French units from de Castries and Langlais at command headquarters.

Nonetheless, the French fought back valiantly. Many members of the garrison were members of the French Foreign Legion, famed for their bravery. Artillerymen risked almost certain death in the open and began to return the Vietminh fire. Riflemen manned the outer barricades of the camp, and, when the Vietminh ground forces attacked, sent them reeling back into the jungle. These barricades were underground bunkers that had been reinforced with a limited supply of timber, and were among the few solid fortifications in the camp. In front of them barbed wire had been strung to delay further a concentrated infantry attack. By dawn General Giap knew that Dien Bien Phu could not be quickly stormed. But he also knew that eventually the French camp could be overrun. He prepared for a relentless siege.

The French garrison had been completely surprised by the ferocity of the Vietminh's opening artillery attack. But de Castries and Langlais were no amateur soldiers. They rallied their men and prepared them for a do-or-die defense stand. They also were able to radio General Navarre for reinforcements since casualties were already severe and would undoubtedly continue to mount. With the airstrip badly damaged and under direct Vietminh artillery fire, the only way these reinforcements could reach Dien Bien Phu was by parachute. In the next few days hundreds of paratroopers landed in the camp, many of whom were dead or wounded by Vietminh fire by the time they hit the ground.

As the siege continued, caring for casualties became a serious problem in the French camp. Originally the plan had been to fly out the wounded. As a result the hospital that had been built had only 44 beds. Within a few weeks there were over 3,000 French wounded. The hospital had only a handful of doctors and medics. It was a grim scene.

In charge of caring for the wounded was a heroic surgeon, Major Paul Grauwin. Major Grauwin worked almost without sleep all through the siege. He was aided by an equally heroic air nurse, Lieutenant Geneviève de Galard-Terraube, the only woman in the French camp. She flew in with a hospital plane and planned to fly out with a load of casualties. When the plane was damaged by shell fire, Lieutenant de Galard-Terraube remained on duty at the hospital throughout the siege. She soon became known as, "The Angel of Dien Bien Phu."

Despite continued French airborne reinforcements, Giap gradually began to close in on Dien Bien Phu. The Vietminh dug tunnels right up to the edge of the French bunkers. From these tunnels Giap's troops would suddenly emerge to engage in fierce hand-to-hand combat with the French. Slowly, and despite enormous Vietminh casualties, one French outpost after another was overrun and the outer perimeter of the camp became smaller and smaller.

The bloody siege went on through March and into April. Gradually it became clear to General Navarre in Saigon and the French government in Paris that Dien Bien Phu was a lost cause. It was at this point that General Ely flew to Washington to ask the United States to mount an airstrike against the Vietminh surrounding Dien Bien Phu.

When General Navarre received word that the United States had refused to enter the war, he relayed this information to de Castries and Langlais at Dien Bien Phu. He also told them that he was sending a relief force from Laos, but it was clear that this was a "too little and too late" gesture. Actually this relief force of about a thousand men never reached the beleaguered garrison, and even if it had, it would have been too small a force to turn the tide of battle.

Day by day and almost foot by foot the Vietminh forces tightened their hold on Dien Bien Phu. De Castries and Langlais refused Giap's offer to let them surrender honorably, and ordered their troops to fight to the last man. On May 1, 1954, Giap began his final mass attack. For a week longer the French managed to hold out, but on May 7 the camp's final few hundred yards were overrun by the Vietminh. Even then fierce hand-to-hand fighting took place before de Castries and Langlais were captured in their command headquarters and were ordered by the Vietminh to tell their troops to surrender.

During the 55 days of battle at Dien Bien Phu the French casualties amounted to 3,000 men killed, more than 5,000 wounded, and about 11,000 captured and marched off to Vietnamese prison camps. During the grim 500-mile march through the jungle to prison camps, several thousand of the French died from exhaustion and exposure. A handful escaped but few of these were heard from again. The few thousand prisoners who survived were released by the Vietminh in August of 1954, following a peace conference agreement at Geneva, Switzerland, on July 20.

Among the French prisoners who survived were both Major Grauwin and Lieutenant de Galard-Terraube. Both were awarded the highest military honors by the French when they returned to France. Later, Major Grauwin returned to Indochina to practice medicine at Phnom Penh in Cambodia.

The Vietminh suffered even heavier casualties than the French during the siege—about 8,000 killed and 15,-

000 wounded. But to Ho Chi Minh and General Giap and especially to the Vietnamese people, the sacrifice was worthwhile. The Vietminh victory at Dien Bien Phu brought an end to France's seven-and-a-half-year effort to regain its empire in Indochina and, at least for a short time, established Vietnamese independence.

Soon after the battle Ho Chi Minh announced that the surviving Vietminh victors at Dien Bien Phu were to be awarded a red-starred button bearing the inscription: *Chien-si Dien Bien* (Combatant of Dien Bien). Vietnamese veterans of that epic battle still proudly wear that badge of honor today.

Unfortunately, Dien Bien Phu started a chain of events that led to the United States' going to war against North Vietnam—a war that was to be the longest and in many ways the most costly in American history. For this reason some historians have said that the Battle of Dien Bien Phu was one of the most important battles in world history. Historian Bernard Fall, for example, has said that the battle "may have done more to shape the fate of the world than the battle of Agincourt, Waterloo, Stalingrad, or Midway."

2.
GENEVA PEACE CONFERENCE: PRELUDE TO WAR

Shortly after Dien Bien Phu fell to the Vietminh, a peace conference was held at Geneva, Switzerland. The purpose of the conference was to get permanent peace settlements in both Korea and Indochina. All of the governments involved in the wars in Southeast Asia attended the meeting. Unfortunately, the conference solved few problems. Instead, it created a major new one.

No solution was found to the Korean situation. The truce there continued—as it does today—but the country remained hopelessly divided. Further, Vietnam was also divided, at the 17th parallel of latitude. This division line was later called the Demilitarized Zone or DMZ. The Vietminh were given control of all territory north of the DMZ, and all territory south of the DMZ was to be controlled by the State of Vietnam, or South Vietnam. This division was only supposed to be temporary; free elections to unify the country were to be held within a year.

Because of its fears about the security of Southeast Asia, the United States reluctantly accepted the Geneva Agreements but did not sign them. The United States

was flatly opposed to any form of Communist government in the area, and the Geneva Agreements left Communists in control of North Vietnam as well as a part of
Laos. A strong South Vietnam, the United States believed, could prevent the further spread of communism.
As a result, President Eisenhower agreed to send several
hundred military advisers to South Vietnam to help train
the South Vietnamese Army.

As soon as the DMZ became a reality, more than a
million North Vietnamese fled into South Vietnam. This
created a serious food shortage which was only eased
when the United States supplied additional economic aid
to South Vietnam.

In 1955 the United States supported the establishment
of South Vietnam as a republic with Ngo Dinh Diem as
its new president. It also supported Diem when he
refused a North Vietnamese request to prepare for the
elections that were to be held to reunify the country.
Diem's refusal was based, he said, on his belief that free
elections were impossible in Communist North Vietnam.
Diem's growing military strength also encouraged him in
his independent actions. He felt that he did not have to
accept any North Vietnamese demands. The Army of the
Republic of Vietnam (ARVN), trained by additional
American military advisers, now numbered more than
150,000 men. Most of them were equipped with up-to-
date U.S. weapons.

Meanwhile, Ho Chi Minh was strengthening North
Vietnam both economically and militarily. Industry ex-
panded, agriculture was improved, and Vietminh military forces were reequipped and resupplied. But this
growth cost many North Vietnamese their lives. Ho Chi
Minh's agriculture improvement program, for example,

was carried out in ruthless fashion. It was aimed basically at redistributing all land to the peasants. When Vietnam had been partitioned, many rich landowners had fled south. However, there were still some people who owned more land than others. Soon the more prosperous landowners were killed or driven from their land, and imprisoned or left to starve. Their land was confiscated and divided up among the poorer peasants. Perhaps as many as 50,000 North Vietnamese died in this purge before a peasant uprising in Ho Chi Minh's home province was put down by General Giap's troops. The land reform program was then somewhat modified.

Behind Ho Chi Minh's harsh measures lay the fact that North Vietnam simply did not produce enough food to feed its people. The best farm land was in the south, which—although he did not openly say so—was one of the reasons why Ho Chi Minh wanted the country reunified. In addition, North Vietnam was not getting massive economic aid the way South Vietnam was.

When President Diem refused to agree to a reunification election, Ho Chi Minh countered with guerrilla raids by northern Vietminh forces into South Vietnam. These northern forces were joined by Vietminh guerrillas who had remained in South Vietnam after the Geneva settlement. By early 1960 the combined Vietminh guerrilla forces grew into a major political and combat organization called the National Liberation Front of South Vietnam, or *Vietcong*. Later in 1960 the entire North Vietnamese organization formed by Ho Chi Minh to "liberate" South Vietnam also became known as the Vietcong. The term means "Vietnamese Communists." The North Vietnamese Army, however, remained a separate and elite combat organization.

The Vietcong's immediate goal was the overthrow of President Diem's government by spreading terrorism throughout South Vietnam. It accomplished its goal by setting up a vast intelligence network that enabled the Vietcong to learn about ARVN troop movements as well as the movements of government officials. Troop movements were then disrupted by sudden Vietcong guerrilla attacks, and the government officials were often kidnapped or assassinated. The Vietcong also bombed public buildings, raided communication centers, and generally caused all kinds of havoc and destruction that would lead to political unrest.

But it was not only the Vietcong who tried to overthrow President Diem's government. Many South Vietnamese were also opposed to it. This was because Diem was in many ways as harsh a dictator as Ho Chi Minh. And Diem's Republic of South Vietnam was a democracy in name only, although its constitution (adopted in 1956) promised equality to the people. In addition, the Diem government was often accused of being corrupt and willing to take bribes in exchange for important jobs and other political favors. Diem was also accused of favoritism toward his family, almost all of whom held high political office. For example, Diem's brother, Ngo Dinh Nhu, who was Diem's chief adviser, was widely accused of bribe-taking.

The major South Vietnamese groups that opposed the Diem regime were various religious groups including the Buddhists, peasant farmers who wanted land redistribution like that in North Vietnam, and even parts of the ARVN or South Vietnamese Army. In the fall of 1960 several battalions of ARVN troops went so far as to surround Diem's Presidential Palace in Saigon, demanding more democratic rule by Diem and his family. Diem promised these reforms and then ordered loyal ARVN troops to put down the minor rebellion. Diem's promised reforms were quickly forgotten.

Despite what was obviously an unsatisfactory situation, the Eisenhower administration continued to back the Diem regime. By 1961 when President John F. Kennedy succeeded Eisenhower as U.S. president there were some 2,000 American military advisers in South Vietnam. Nevertheless, Eisenhower was uneasy about America's continued commitment to Diem's despotic rule. Further assignment of American military advisers to South Vietnam could lead to the major land war in Southeast Asia that Eisenhower had long feared. On inauguration day Eisenhower warned Kennedy that he might have to send troops to Indochina. Once in office, Kennedy seriously considered such action, but shied away from actually doing so. Nevertheless, during the Kennedy administration the number of American military advisers in South Vietnam was to increase to 15,000, and the United States would find itself on the brink of a major, undeclared war.

Kennedy did not want to involve the United States in a Vietnam war, or a war of any kind for that matter. But neither did he want the United States simply to get out of Vietnam. Like Presidents Truman and Eisenhower before him, Kennedy believed in the so-called "Domino Theory." This meant that if one country fell to the Communists all of the other countries in the area would also topple over to them like a series of dominoes. It was a theory that would be held by two future U.S. presidents, Lyndon Johnson and Richard Nixon. Thus, five American presidents, Truman, Eisenhower, Kennedy, Johnson, and Nixon, would all bear at least partial responsibility for America's role in the Vietnam tragedy.

But there was more than merely the domino theory behind America's involvement in Vietnam. The theory itself grew out of the "Cold War" between the United States and the Soviet Union, which had begun shortly after the end of World War II.

During World War II the United States and the Soviet Union had been allies. After this conflict ended with the defeat of Hitler's Germany, the United States and its other major wartime ally, Great Britain, began to fear that Russia would try to dominate the whole of Europe. On the other hand, Soviet dictator Joseph Stalin believed that Russia was now threatened by both Britain and the United States. Stalin especially feared the United States because it was the only country with the atom bomb at its disposal.

Despite Anglo-American reassurances to the contrary, Stalin feared that his country might be attacked again, just as it had been attacked in World War II by Hitler's Germany (with whom Russia had also had the reassurance of a non-aggression pact). As Russia began to recover from its enormous war losses, Stalin began an aggressive campaign to take over control of nations that bordered on the Soviet Union. These Communist-controlled or satellite nations would, he felt, form a buffer against any future invasion. Britain's Winston Churchill warned Stalin against stretching an "iron curtain" across Europe, but Stalin ignored the warning and Soviet expansion continued.

U.S. President Franklin Roosevelt had hoped to avoid all future world wars with the establishment of the

United Nations in 1945. The ideals of this peace-keeping organization were also supported by Roosevelt's successor, Harry Truman. They included free elections and self-determination by all nations, and the negotiated settlements of all future conflicts between nations.

Stalin, however, had little or no faith in the United Nations. He had seen how weak and unimportant a similar international peace organization, the League of Nations, had been after World War I. The League of Nations had failed to prevent World War II, and Stalin expected the United Nations to be equally powerless. He continued to build up the strength of the Russian army and urged Soviet scientists to speed up their efforts to produce an atomic bomb. Also a network of Soviet spies within the United States was ordered to investigate the secrets of how the atom bomb was made.

In an effort to counter Soviet aggression in Europe President Truman declared "that it must be the policy of the United States to support free peoples who are resisting attempted subjugation by armed, outside pressures." This was called the Truman Doctrine. In addition to freedom-seeking European nations it was soon applied to freedom-seeking nations in Indochina and elsewhere throughout the world.

Out of the Truman Doctrine grew the Marshall Plan, which was named for U.S. Secretary of State George C. Marshall. Under the Marshall Plan war-ravaged nations were offered massive economic aid by the United States to speed their recovery. Many European nations took advantage of this offer which proved to be a key reason for the post-World War II economic recovery of Europe.

Stalin, however, refused offers of Marshall Plan aid and ordered all Soviet satellite nations to refuse it. The

Marshall Plan, Stalin insisted, would make "capitalist slaves out of those who took the money." When several satellite countries threatened to ignore Stalin's orders, their governments were replaced with Communist dictatorships. The former allies of World War II, the United States and the Soviet Union, were now clearly involved in a grim Cold War. It reached a peak in 1948 with the "Berlin Blockade."

At the end of World War II the victorious allies divided Germany in half. Russia took over East Germany and ran it as a Communist puppet state or Soviet satellite. West Germany was established as an independent and democratic republic. Berlin, the prewar capital of Germany, was partitioned into eastern and western sectors, with Russia controlling the eastern sector and France, Great Britain, and the United States occupying the western sector. Berlin, however, was located in Soviet-dominated East Germany. Access to West Berlin was allowed by the Russians along a narrow corridor running through East Germany.

In 1948 Russia blockaded the corridor leading to West Berlin. The Western allies, principally Great Britain and the United States, responded by flying supplies into West Berlin. This blockade lasted for almost a year until the Soviets finally realized that the airlift could not be stopped by any measures short of war. The blockade was then lifted.

In 1949 the Soviet Union exploded its first atom bomb. The ending of America's nuclear monopoly made Russia even more aggressive, and Stalin began to issue new threats against the Western allies. These included the possibility of taking over the whole of Berlin and even West Germany.

To counter these threats the principal nations of Western Europe, along with the United States and Canada, formed the North Atlantic Treaty Organization (NATO). NATO was effective in containing the Soviet Union both economically and militarily, and for the next several years the Cold War became something of a stalemate. Neither side was able to gain an advantage over the other.

Meanwhile in Asia, Mao Tse-tung and the Chinese Communist Army took over control of the whole of mainland China, establishing the People's Republic of China in 1949. Chiang Kai-shek and his Nationalists were forced onto the island of Formosa (Taiwan) and were supported by the United States in their claims to the legitimate government of China. Communist uprisings were also taking place in the Philippines, Malaya, Burma, and in Vietnam where they were led by Ho Chi Minh and his Vietminh forces.

In the United States many people regarded these Communist efforts in Europe and Asia as an international conspiracy on the part of the Soviet Union to conquer the world. When North Korea, backed by Russia and Red China, attacked South Korea in June of 1950, these "conspiracy" theorists had their worst suspicions confirmed.

Further confirmation of a suspected Soviet international conspiracy was found by many in the several Communist spy trials that were held in the United States. These trials left little doubt that the Soviet spy network in the United States had successfully breached American secrecy surrounding methods for making atom bombs. Soon accusations of treason were widespread even in the highest ranks of American government.

These accusations reached their peak of vicious unreality between 1950 and 1954 when Republican Senator Joseph McCarthy of Wisconsin accused the U.S. State Department of harboring Communists. McCarthy's allegations that Communists had also infiltrated other departments of the government, as well as American education and the defense industries, created a mood of national hysteria that had not been matched since the witch trials at Salem, Massachusetts, in the early days of the country.

There was little doubt that some secrets had been stolen and turned over to Russia. But McCarthy's claim that treasonable activities were widespread was clearly ridiculous. This became evident when it was shown that McCarthy had little or no evidence to back up his accusations. Nevertheless, many loyal Americans had their reputations and their careers destroyed before the hysteria ended.

McCarthy did not confine his accusations to the domestic scene. During the Korean War he suspected that some of America's United Nations allies were shipping strategic war materials to China for use by North Korea. McCarthy promptly demanded in front of news cameras: "Let us sink every accursed ship carrying materials to the enemy and resulting in the death of American boys, regardless of what flags those ships fly." One of the countries accused by McCarthy of such treacherous action was Great Britain. Since British and British Commonwealth boys were fighting and dying right alongside American boys in Korea, the McCarthy accusation was somewhat suspect, to say the least.

Finally, in 1954, McCarthy was censured by his Senate colleagues. He died in 1957.

Long after McCarthy's death, however, many Americans continued to believe in the threat of an international Communist conspiracy. Even the death of Stalin in 1953 and the Korean War armistice that same year did not end the Cold War.

To prevent Communist expansion, the United States continued to give massive aid to both European and Asian countries opposed to Communism. In Asia the United States was able to get a number of anticommunist nations to band together in the South East Asia Treaty Organization (SEATO), similar to NATO in Europe. Each SEATO nation was supposed to go to the aid of the other if one of them was threatened by a Communist take-over. But when the government of South Vietnam was threatened by North Vietnamese Communists, no SEATO nation other than the United States at first came to South Vietnam's aid. Later Australia and New Zealand sent token forces.

Many people in the United States could not understand the lack of support. They refused to accept the possibility that the revolutionary movements in Southeast Asia might be both nationalist as well as Communist movements. That any freedom-seeking nations would voluntarily choose communism rather than democracy seemed highly unlikely to most Americans. Human liberty and communism, they felt, were simply an impossible combination.

A few months after Kennedy took office in January 1961 he was faced with a Cold War crisis. The crisis occurred off the southern shores of the United States in Cuba. Communist Fidel Castro had taken over as dictator of Cuba in 1959. In an effort to overthrow Castro, the U.S. Central Intelligence Agency (CIA) had planned an invasion of Cuba by Cuban refugees living in the United States. This mission had been planned before Kennedy became president, but he agreed that it should proceed.

When the invasion took place at Cuba's Bay of Pigs in the spring of 1961, it was a disastrous failure. Castro's military forces were ready and waiting for the American-trained and American-equipped refugees when they landed, and drove them back into the sea.

Embarrassed by this fiasco, Kennedy made it clear he would adopt a hard line in all future dealings with Communist governments. He did not have long to wait for a new Communist challenge.

In June 1961 Kennedy met in Vienna, Austria, with Nikita Khrushchev, who had succeeded Stalin as Russia's dictator. The stated purpose of the meeting was to slow down the arms race between the East and West. But Khrushchev adopted a belligerent attitude and told Kennedy that the Western allies should get out of Berlin. Although Khrushchev did not mention the fact, thousands of people annually were fleeing from East Berlin into West Berlin, and this angered Soviet leaders.

Kennedy, of course, refused to abandon Berlin. Shortly after he returned to Washington the Russians began erecting a wall across Berlin, cutting the city in half. Its purpose was to prevent further escapes by people fleeing from Communist East Berlin. When the United States accepted the Berlin Wall, Khrushchev dropped his demands that the West leave the city.

But Kennedy soon faced another direct and potentially more dangerous conflict with Khrushchev. This conflict again involved Cuba.

After the abortive United States-sponsored invasion of Cuba, Castro had called upon the Soviet Union for aid in defending his country against future attack. Khrushchev responded to Castro's request by offering to install in Cuba Soviet rockets equipped with nuclear warheads. These rockets could shift the balance of terror in Russia's favor because they would threaten U.S. cities with attack. Castro accepted the offer, and the secret installation of the rockets began in the autumn of 1962.

Aerial reconnaissance by American planes disclosed the rocket installations, and Kennedy immediately demanded that they be removed. The challenge reached its climax when Kennedy ordered the U.S. Navy to intercept Soviet ships carrying rockets for the installations. The world held its breath as the rocket-laden ships approached Cuba. Many Americans watched the confrontation on television. At the last moment Khrushchev ordered the Soviet ships to turn back, and the world breathed a sigh of relief at its narrow escape from possible nuclear destruction.

This atmosphere of Cold War confrontation was present throughout Kennedy's first two years in office. It strongly influenced his decisions about America's continued presence in Vietnam.

In the spring of 1961 President Kennedy sent his vice-president, Lyndon Johnson, to South Vietnam to check on its economic and military condition. Later Kennedy's military adviser, General Maxwell Taylor, was sent on a similar mission. Both men reported that, due to increasing Vietcong guerrilla raids and President Diem's refusal to reform his despotic rule, the government of South Vietnam was in danger of collapse. The United States Central Intelligence Agency (CIA) also reported widespread corruption in the Diem government.

Nevertheless, Kennedy decided to continue U.S. support of Diem largely because Diem's overthrow might result in anarchy, with no one in control of the country. For a time Kennedy considered sending combat troops to South Vietnam, but he settled instead for several thousand additional military advisers and increased economic aid. Kennedy hoped that this additional support would boost the morale of the South Vietnamese Army (ARVN) and persuade President Diem to be more cooperative in establishing a truly democratic government.

Diem gladly accepted the additional thousands of military advisers and some $400 million worth of military equipment and supplies during the next two years. But his rule remained as dictatorial as ever. In addition, Diem's much-criticized brother and also his sister-in-law, Madame Ngo Dinh Nhu, continued to act like autocratic members of a royal family, passing out special privileges and giving high-level government jobs to their favorites. These actions further aroused the anger of the South Vietnamese people.

A crisis occurred in the spring of 1963 when President Diem, a Roman Catholic, refused to let the Buddhists fly flags in the city of Hue on Buddha's birthday. Riots broke out in Hue and spread to Saigon, South Vietnam's capital. ARVN troops attempted to put down the riots in Saigon and thousands of Buddhists were arrested. Some of those arrested were later tortured and killed.

In protest Buddhist priests publicly burned themselves to death in Saigon by pouring gasoline on their robes and setting themselves on fire. These ritual suicides outraged the public in both South Vietnam and the United States, where pictures of them appeared in newspapers as well as on television. President Kennedy, through the American ambassador in Saigon, demanded that President Diem make peace with the Buddhists by announcing a policy of religious equality. Diem was about to do so when Madame Ngo Dinh Nhu denounced the Buddhists as traitors and Communists. Madame Nhu, whom newspaper correspondents called "The Dragon Lady," even went a step further: she told reporters that she applauded every time "one of those so-called holy men put on a barbecue show."

In the midst of the furor that followed, the Vietcong launched new guerrilla attacks on South Vietnam, some of which penetrated as far as Saigon itself. Desertions from the South Vietnamese Army increased, and there were widespread threats of ARVN mutiny.

Early in November President Diem and his brother, Ngo Dinh Nhu, were driven from the Presidential Palace, captured, and assassinated by a group of ARVN generals. These generals, probably aided by the CIA, then took over control of the government.

Later that same month President Kennedy was assassinated while on a political tour in Dallas, Texas. Attempting to bring order out of the chaos of the United States' involvement in Vietnam was now up to the new president, Lyndon Baines Johnson.

3.
INCIDENT IN THE
GULF OF TONKIN:
THE WAR BEGINS

After the assassination of President Diem a regular parade of heads of government began in South Vietnam. In fact it would not be until several years later, with the election of General Nguyen Van Thieu as president in 1967, that the parade would draw to a halt. However, each of the five leaders who succeeded Diem was given support by the United States.

The first South Vietnamese leader supported by the Lyndon Johnson administration was General Nguyen Khanh. Johnson told Khanh that in return for $60 million in additional war material and economic aid, he expected the ARVN forces to be increased by 50,000 men in order to combat the Vietcong who by that time controlled almost half of South Vietnam. This Khanh agreed to do, but he made little effort to live up to his promise. Instead, Khanh and General Nguyen Cao Ky, commander of the South Vietnamese Air Force, began demanding that both land and air attacks be made by American forces against North Vietnam.

In an effort to pressure the United States into action, General Ky made a public announcement that American military forces had actually been secretly engaged in combat against the Vietcong for some time. Although the Johnson administration stoutly denied Ky's statement, it was nevertheless true.

Beginning in 1961—during the Kennedy administration—the American military "advisers" had included a number of Army Special Forces soldiers who had fought and died in battle against the Vietcong. In fact the first American soldier to die in Vietnam was killed in a Vietcong road ambush near Saigon in December of 1961. He was Specialist 4th Class James Thomas Davis, twenty-five, from Livingston, Tennessee.

Davis, like all of the other members of the U.S. Army's Special Forces, was trained in antiguerrilla (officially called "counterinsurgency") warfare. (Vietcong guerrillas were regarded as insurgents or rebels against lawful authority by the United States.) Members of the Special Forces were experts in jungle fighting, sabotage, and various other activities to harass the Vietcong. They were also trained as paratroopers so they could be parachuted into remote, Vietcong-occupied jungle areas. There they worked with local village governments in recruiting and training local citizens as antiguerrilla soldiers. They then led these soldiers into battle against the Vietcong. Many Special Forces soldiers worked in South Vietnam's Central Highlands with mountain tribes called *Montagnards.*

Members of the Special Forces were called "Green Berets" because of the distinctive green berets they wore as symbols of their unique branch of military service. The Green Berets were great favorites of President Kennedy's, perhaps because of their courageous and romantic reputation as devil-may-care fighters. As a patrol boat (PT) skipper in World War II, Kennedy had been called upon to display a similar kind of lone-wolf courage. He was so fascinated by the Green Berets that he once had his brother Robert invite a unit of them to the grounds of the Kennedy family home at Hyannisport, Massachusetts, to exhibit their guerrilla skills. Later, when President Kennedy authorized the sending of several thousand additional military advisers to Vietnam in 1962, he made certain that at least 200 of them were Green Berets. This number was steadily increased under both Kennedy and Johnson.

Under President Johnson what amounted to aerial warfare was being carried on in secret against the Vietcong. American pilots with orders to fire back if fired upon flew reconnaissance missions over Vietcong territory—especially the Ho Chi Minh Trail in Laos. Green Beret teams were flown in and out of combat areas, and naval "frogmen" were dropped from hovering helicopters off the North Vietnamese coast where they could swim ashore and sabotage Vietcong coastal installations.

While he was openly denying all claims of such American secret, or covert, activity, President Johnson was busy increasing it. Early in 1964, after the fall of Diem, the covert bombing of Laos near the North Vietnamese border was begun. Johnson also authorized hit-and-run commando raids by South Vietnamese PT boats against North Vietnamese naval bases, and ordered U.S. Navy destroyers to patrol the North Vietnamese coast "to gather intelligence information." In the summer of 1964 Johnson had his staff prepare a resolution to present to the United States Congress that would permit the open use of American military forces against North Vietnam.

On July 31 South Vietnamese PT boats attacked two

North Vietnamese naval bases on the Gulf of Tonkin. The next day the United States destroyer *Maddox* sailed along the coast, trying to detect North Vietnamese radar installations. Intercepted radio messages made it clear that the Vietcong thought both missions were a part of the same hostile operation, although U.S. officials later denied this. On August 2 the *Maddox* was attacked by three North Vietnamese PT boats. The *Maddox* escaped undamaged after sinking one of the attacking boats. Captain John Herrick, commander of the Tonkin Gulf Patrol, cabled Washington suggesting that any further such patrols would be "an unacceptable risk." But the next day, as a show of strength, the *Maddox* was ordered back on patrol duty in the Gulf of Tonkin. Accompanying the *Maddox* was another U.S. destroyer, the *C. Turner Joy.*

The events surrounding this second destroyer patrol were not too clear. In fact controversy still surrounds them. On August 4 Captain Herrick radioed Washington that both destroyers were under attack and that the North Vietnamese thought the warlike action by the United States was part of the original mission begun several days earlier. What was not clear was whether the two American destroyers had actually been fired upon by the North Vietnamese. Later the possibility arose that crews on the two destroyers had made a mistake and the American ships had begun firing at each other. Some U.S. intelligence officers even claimed that an inexperienced radar operator aboard the *Maddox* had mistaken "blips" on his radar screen for enemy PT boats when they had actually been caused by the wake of the *C. Turner Joy.*

New York Times correspondent David Halberstam reported that when President Johnson was asked some months later what had actually happened in the Gulf of Tonkin on August 4, 1964, Johnson said with a grin: "For all I know, our Navy was shooting at whales out there."

Nevertheless, at the time both Johnson and the destroyer crews seemed to be convinced that U.S. warships were being attacked by the North Vietnamese. Although the destroyers escaped unharmed, their gunners claimed they sank two of the attacking North Vietnamese PT boats and damaged two others.

The next day Johnson ordered retaliatory air strikes against the PT boat bases. Flying from the U.S. aircraft carriers *Ticonderoga* and *Constellation,* American fighter-bombers reportedly destroyed some 25 PT boats at their North Vietnamese bases, as well as a nearby oil refinery. Two American planes were shot down by antiaircraft fire.

Fearing that any stronger U.S. action might bring China or even Russia into the conflict, Johnson made it clear that this was a "carefully measured response" and that he wanted no wider war. At the same time, however, he sought authority from Congress to widen the war if necessary. On August 7 Congress gave him this authority by passing the Gulf of Tonkin Resolution, which Johnson signed on August 11. This resolution was not a declaration of war, but it had much the same effect. It gave Johnson complete authority "to take all necessary measures to repel any armed attack against the forces of the United States and to take all necessary steps including the use of armed force to assist" South Vietnam or any other member of the South East Asia Treaty Organization.

Only two U.S. senators voted against the Gulf of Tonkin Resolution. They were Ernest Gruening of Alaska and Wayne Morse of Oregon. On the day the resolution was passed Morse said prophetically: "I believe that history will record that we have made a great mistake in subverting and circumventing the Constitution of the United States by means of this resolution. We are in effect giving the president warmaking powers in the absence of a declaration of war. I believe that to be a mistake."

But Morse's words went unheeded by most Americans, and certainly by President Lyndon Johnson. He now had the legal authority to wage war against what he described as a "raggedy-ass little fourth-rate country." And on the eve of his contest for reelection as president —his opponent was Senator Barry Goldwater of Arizona —Johnson had never stood higher in the public opinion polls.

On November 3, 1964, Lyndon Johnson was reelected United States president in a landslide victory over Barry Goldwater. Johnson's 43 million votes to Goldwater's 27 million gave Johnson 61 percent of the vote, the largest percentage ever received by an American president up to that time.

But Johnson was a shrewd enough politician and judge of the American people to know that his landslide victory did not give him a mandate to expand the United States' role in Vietnam to any great extent. In fact one of the reasons Johnson had won so decisively was that in the months following the Gulf of Tonkin incident he had skillfully played down any further American action. He had also said, "We are not about to send American boys nine or ten thousand miles away from home to do what

Asian boys ought to be doing for themselves." At the same time his campaign strategy had been to picture Goldwater as a warmonger who would not hesitate to involve the United States in a nuclear war in Southeast Asia.

However, like all of America's Vietnam wartime presidents, Johnson was caught in the trap of the Vietnam conflict. During his long years in the Senate before moving into the executive branch of government, Johnson had an admirable record as a legislator. His ability to persuade other senators to vote for social welfare measures had made him a key figure in the passage of numerous pieces of legislation that benefited the entire nation. As president he wanted nothing more than to concentrate on important domestic issues, but the Vietnam issue simply would not go away. He was held captive by it.

Nevertheless, in spite of Vietnam, Johnson did manage to get much important domestic legislation enacted during his first year in office. Much of the groundwork for this legislation had been laid by the Kennedy administration, but it was Johnson who got it passed by the Congress. It included a major bill aiding education, public works legislation, and the most far-reaching civil rights bill in the nation's history.

President Kennedy had called his administration's domestic program "the New Frontier." In carrying on and expanding the Kennedy domestic program, Johnson called his "the Great Society." Its goals were centered on antipoverty, health, education, conservation, and urban planning measures. Congress approved many of Johnson's proposals, but more and more the Vietnam situation overshadowed domestic issues.

By the end of 1964 American military advisory strength in South Vietnam had increased somewhat to a total of about 25,000 men. However, early in 1965 these advisers were released for combat and the troop buildup began. Small contingents of troops from South Korea, Australia, and New Zealand also arrived to help fight against the Vietcong. Eventually Thailand, Taiwan, and the Philippines would contribute troops also.

Johnson, of course, wanted to be done with the war. His advisers told him that it was possible, but first political stability would have to be established in South Vietnam.

Johnson's chief advisers at this time were Secretary of State Dean Rusk, Secretary of Defense Robert McNamara, Ambassador to South Vietnam General Maxwell Taylor, and Commander of the U.S. Military Forces in Vietnam General William Westmoreland. Westmoreland was not in favor of a major air offensive unless it was accompanied by a large increase in American ground troops. The Joint Chiefs of Staff of the army, navy, and air force, who also advised the president on specific military actions, were inclined to agree with Westmoreland—at least insofar as the troop buildup was concerned.

Establishing any kind of political stability in South Vietnam, however, was much easier said than done. Plots and counterplots by South Vietnamese generals and renewed conflict between Catholic and Buddhist factions brought South Vietnam to the brink of civil war. Meanwhile, Vietcong guerrillas launched bold terrorist attacks against newly established American military bases in the countryside, as well as against administrative installations—including the American Embassy in Saigon. Hundreds of American and South Vietnamese soldiers and civilians were killed or wounded in these attacks.

In retaliation American air raids on a limited scale were launched against North Vietnam. President Johnson did not let the public know until early in 1965 that American pilots were flying the planes engaged in these raids. The main targets were highways and bridges. Bombers also struck the Ho Chi Minh Trail in neighboring Laos, and U.S. warships shelled key North Vietnamese coastal installations.

But the Vietcong failed to respond to these American reprisals. Consequently, President Johnson resorted to his "Ouch Theory": if "Uncle Ho" was hit hard enough, he was supposed to cry, "Ouch!" and quit the war. (Sometimes this was also called the "Uncle Theory"— Ho Chi Minh would cry "Uncle" if he was hit hard enough.) To test his theory Johnson agreed to the launching of a major aerial-bombing offensive against North Vietnam. Called "Operation Rolling Thunder," this air war began in the spring of 1965 and was to last until the fall of 1968. During the course of Operation Rolling Thunder there were occasional brief pauses to try to get peace negotiations under way, but Ho Chi Minh made it clear that United States forces would have to be withdrawn from South Vietnam before such negotiations could begin. The bombing of North Vietnam was then resumed with fighter-bombers taking off from U.S. aircraft carriers and South Vietnamese airfields and B-52 strategic bombers taking off from as far away as Guam.

On March 8, 1965, at the same time that Operation Rolling Thunder was being launched, a major contingent of U.S. Marines hit the beaches at Da Nang. There was already an American airfield at Da Nang, and the several battalions of Marine infantrymen plus artillery support were brought in to protect it from Vietcong attack. The newly arrived Marine Expeditionary Brigade, however, met with no opposition when it landed. Instead, its members were greeted by South Vietnamese girls who placed necklaces of flowers called *leis* around their necks. But within a matter of weeks the marines would be faced with fierce Vietcong guerrilla attacks.

Later in the spring the U.S. Army's 173rd Airborne Brigade landed in South Vietnam, and on July 28 President Johnson made an historic announcement at a nationally televised press conference: "I have today ordered to Vietnam the First Cavalry Airmobile Division and certain other forces, which will raise our fighting strength to almost 125,000 men almost immediately." He added, "Additional forces will be needed, and they will be sent as requested."

Up to this point President Johnson had been able to manage the war without letting the American people know what was really going on. Now he was open about it, and there could be little doubt in anybody's mind that the United States government was totally committed to the Vietnam War.

In August these troops began pouring into Vietnam—not the 125,000 Johnson had originally estimated, but closer to 175,000. Before 1965 ended the number approached 200,000 U.S. combat troops, and the end was not in sight.

General William C. Westmoreland, commander of allied forces in Vietnam, awards a medal to a First Infantry Division officer. *U.S. Army Photo*

(LEFT) Marine General Lewis W. Walt talks over combat plans with ARVN General Hoang Xuan Lam. *Defense Department Photo* (RIGHT) Ho Chi Minh, President of the Democratic Republic of (North) Vietnam. *UPI Photo*

U.S. destroyer *C. Turner Joy. U.S. Navy Photo*

A U.S. nuclear-powered aircraft carrier alongside a supply ship in the Gulf of Tonkin. *U.S. Navy Photo*

U.S. military advisers training their South Vietnamese allies. *U.S. Navy Photo*

South Vietnamese combat forces are transported into coastal combat by a U.S. patrol boat. *U.S. Navy Photo*

Wearing camouflage paint and camouflage clothing, members of a U.S. and South Vietnamese naval sea, air, and land (SEAL) team prepare for a secret mission against the enemy. Navy SEAL teams, like the army's Green Berets, specialized in unconventional, antiguerrilla, or counterinsurgency warfare. *U.S. Navy Photo*

A Vietnamese farmer is questioned by an ARVN soldier about the possibility of Vietcong in the local village. *U.S. Army Photo*

A First Division grunt tries to sleep in the rain after a combat mission while his buddy remains on guard. *UPI Photo*

A wounded U.S. soldier is rushed from a rescue helicopter to a base field hospital. *U.S. Army Photo*

South Vietnamese soldiers and American advisers move supplies from a helicopter under Vietcong fire. *Defense Department Photo*

American infantrymen are "helilifted" into combat. *U.S. Army Photo*

A combat patrol moves along a trail in the Central Highlands. *U.S. Army Photo*

A U.S. mortar team in action. *U.S. Army Photo*

Army troops fire on the Vietcong. *U.S. Air Force Photo*

U.S. forces storm a hill held by the Vietcong near the DMZ. *Defense Department Photo*

4.
UNCONVENTIONAL VIETCONG WARFARE, CONVENTIONAL U.S. METHODS

In 1965 the war against North Vietnam became an American war. And in waging it the United States military forces ran head on into the same major problem that had plagued the French: the inability, except on rare occasions, to force the Vietcong to concentrate their combat forces into single large infantry units and fight traditional set piece battles. Guerrilla warfare had been successful against the French, and General Giap saw no reason why it shouldn't be successful against the Americans. United States military leaders, of course, were certain that superior American ability, manpower, technology, and firepower could solve this problem.

The capacity of superior American technology and firepower to end the war quickly had its first major test in Operation Rolling Thunder. Unlimited aerial bombing had proved inconclusive in both World War II and the Korean War. Or, if it had proved anything at all, it had proved that people subjected to it became more determined than ever to defeat those responsible for the bombing. But this time, declared American leaders from President Johnson on down, it would be a different story.

When plans for wide-scale area bombing were first made, air force generals said that the Vietcong leaders at Hanoi could be brought to their knees in a month—perhaps six weeks at the most. But six weeks of the aerial offensive passed, and then six months, and the Vietcong seemed undisturbed. Men and supplies kept pouring into South Vietnam, the soldiers moving not as large, single units but as infiltrators in groups of two or three or half a dozen. Once in South Vietnam, these small groups of infiltrators joined several others in guerrilla teams to stage hit-and-run attacks. They were usually kept supplied by streams of porters pushing cargo-laden bicycles. When this source failed, the Vietcong simply took over local villages and confiscated food supplies. As often as not the villagers proved to be Vietcong sympathizers.

During 1965 the U.S. Air Force dropped more bombs on Vietnam than it had dropped in the Pacific theater of war in World War II. By 1967 it had dropped more bombs than it had dropped in the European theater of war. By the time Operation Rolling Thunder was abandoned in 1968 the U.S. Air Force had dropped more bombs on Vietnam than had been dropped by both the Allies and the Axis powers in the whole of World War II.

And still the Vietcong, their morale high, kept coming.

The Vietcong forces infiltrating South Vietnam were hidden from American planes beneath the jungle roof—just as the troops and the porters who carried supplies to General Giap's forces at Dien Bien Phu were hidden from French aerial observation and attack. The U.S. Air Force sprayed a weed-killer called Agent Orange to kill all of the leaves on the jungle trees. Vast areas of tropical forests were destroyed in this futile effort to disclose

Vietcong infiltration trails and encampments. In the process much peasant farmland was rendered useless for rice and other crops.

Napalm, an explosive petroleum jelly, was also dropped over areas suspected of hiding Vietcong infiltrators. The flames from this fiercely burning jelly destroyed thousands of acres of jungle and countless Vietnamese thatched villages as well.

There was little doubt that United States industrial might could produce superior technology and firepower. But it could not destroy Vietcong staying power.

The U.S. Air Force also tried to halt the flow of Vietcong weapons, ammunition, and food at their source. If this could be done, the Vietcong soldiers in South Vietnam would eventually perish. This part of Operation Rolling Thunder called for the strategic precision bombing of the city of Hanoi and the port of Haiphong, through which flowed supplies from China and Russia.

Success in cutting off the source of Vietcong supplies was hampered by several factors. First of all, the Johnson administration was fearful that China and Russia would enter the war. Therefore, to avoid provoking the Chinese, railroads on the Chinese mainland leading from China into Hanoi could not be bombed. Railroad bridges just outside Hanoi could, of course, be bombed, but these bridges were heavily protected by antiaircraft sites. To avoid provoking the Russians, extreme care had to be taken in bombing Haiphong harbor because Soviet supply ships were frequently anchored there.

Second, Hanoi had no vast military industrial complex such as Germany's Ruhr Valley in World War II. In fact there were no vast, vulnerable targets in the whole of North Vietnam. Hanoi did have a large steel mill and several oil refineries which were destroyed, but North Vietnam's needs from these sources were soon resupplied by China and Russia.

Finally, American technology was well matched by the defensive fighter aircraft and radar-directed antiaircraft weaponry put in the hands of the Vietcong by the Soviet Union.

The Soviet-built MiG interceptor aircraft flown by the North Vietnamese was an excellent plane that had proved its worth in the Korean War. In Korea, in 1950, it and American F-80 Shooting Stars had engaged in the first jet plane combat in history. American flyers had learned to respect the MiG in Korea, and this respect grew in Vietnam. North Vietnamese pilots, many of them trained by the Chinese, were not as experienced as American pilots, but they learned rapidly and soon became formidable foes. In the first aerial combat between American and North Vietnamese aircraft in 1965, two U.S. F-105 Thunderchief fighter-bombers were shot down by MiG-17 interceptors.

Still, the most fearsome of North Vietnamese defenses against aerial bombardment were the Soviet-built antiaircraft batteries and surface-to-air missile (SAM) sites. The SAM was a kind of highly sophisticated aerial torpedo launched from the ground. Electronically operated, it had a radar screen that picked up approaching enemy planes and a built-in computer that figured out precise target data, including the direction and angle the SAM should take. After the SAM was launched it could be guided by radio and thus it could often track a plane taking evasive action. The only type of maneuver that could outwit a SAM was sudden and violent evasive action, but this meant that a pilot had to see the approaching missile from some distance. A SAM fired from the ground through heavy cloud cover was virtually unavoidable since it would be impossible for a pilot to see it before it hit.

SAM sites were vulnerable to low-level aerial attack which avoided detection by radar. But such attacks exposed the American aircraft to fire from the antiaircraft guns that protected all SAM sites. North Vietnamese antiaircraft batteries were also electronically operated and radar guided. They could be operated manually as well, however, and poured forth a hail of .37 millimeter shells at a rate of 180 rounds per minute. Small arms fire and machine guns also proved surprisingly effective against American planes on long, low-level bombing runs against SAM and antiaircraft gun sites. The United States gradually developed an antiradar missile called the Shrike which could be fired from an attacking plane, but in the end quick, dive-bombing attacks proved to be the most successful method of knocking out SAM sites. Nevertheless, no matter what method was used to attack the SAM sites, the U.S. casualty rate remained high.

Often downed American flyers were rescued before they could be taken prisoner by the Vietcong. Helicopters played a key role in such rescue missions. One of the most successful of these was the huge Sikorsky HH-3, which was commonly called, "The Jolly Green Giant." Flying out of Thailand, where they were stationed, these versatile aircraft and their courageous crews saved hundreds of flyers from capture and imprisonment. Downed flyers were frequently snatched from the midst of enemy defense troops on suicidal rescue missions.

Air force, army, navy, and marine helicopters were used so extensively in the Vietnam conflict that it was often called, "The 'Chopper' War." The workhorse choppers for the army were the Chinook and various kinds of Bell helicopters, which were used for rescue operations, but mainly to airlift troops into and out of combat. The navy flew modified Sikorsky Sea King anti-submarine choppers on rescue missions both on land and in the Gulf of Tonkin, into which American flyers frequently parachuted after ejecting from their badly damaged planes. Marine choppers also were used for rescue work and to airlift troops into battle. The Bell "Huey" was one of the most widely used combat helicopters by both the marines and the navy.

The wide use of helicopters by all of the U.S. military forces in Vietnam, however, was in a large sense self-defeating. The ability it gave troops to range quickly over vast areas gave the Americans the illusion that they were somehow in control of these areas, when really they were not. The versatile chopper fulfilled the need for controlling affairs by machinery and other technology. The end result was that the machinery was actually controlling the American military and how it fought the war.

Taking over and maintaining control of the Vietnam countryside was a constant problem for U.S. ground forces. The first major ground combat between American troops and the Vietcong took place in August of 1965. This occurred when several thousand U.S. Marines attacked an equal number of Vietcong on a peninsula that jutted into the South China Sea along the north-central coast where the Vietcong were threatening an American airfield.

It was one of the rare times when the Vietcong were concentrated in a relatively large number, and the marines took full advantage of the opportunity. Landing on the peninsula by sea and air, the marines quickly routed the Vietcong, killing more than 700 of them. Marine losses were 50 killed and 150 wounded. The defeated Vietcong fled into the nearby hills and jungle.

Clearly "Operation Starlite," as Marine General Lewis Walt named the battle, was a marine victory. However, no U.S. forces were available to occupy the peninsula, and in a few weeks the Vietcong had reoccupied it. Once again the marines were called upon to drive them out, and the same kind of see-saw fighting continued for months and years with the United States never really gaining the upper hand.

Operation Starlite was typical of the major American and Vietcong infantry action throughout the war. It was an example of why General Westmoreland continued to call for more and more troops, despite the fact that the United States could not possibly supply enough manpower to occupy the whole of Vietnam or even the portion of it temporarily taken over by U.S. forces.

In an attempt to solve the problem, General Westmoreland devised two combat techniques. One was called "Search and Destroy," and the other was known as the "Free Fire Zone."

In the "Search and Destroy" method army infantry brigades and divisions would establish permanent base camps throughout South Vietnam. A certain number of men would always be left on duty to defend these base camps. These were called "security forces." Then, leaving the security forces behind, several companies of infantry would move off into the jungles surrounding the base camps. There they would build temporary bases supported by artillery. From these temporary bases the infantry GIs, or "grunts" as they proudly called themselves, would sweep through the jungles on armed patrols in search of Vietcong whom they would try to destroy.

Because Vietcong moving into South Vietnam from the north frequently occupied local villages, there often appeared to be no way of driving them out without killing villagers in the process. To prevent this General Westmoreland decided to relocate the local civilians, declare the villages "Free Fire Zones," and then destroy the villages with artillery barrages. The Vietcong, of course, would disappear into the surrounding jungles as soon as the Americans began to relocate the local civilians, but the destruction of the villages would prevent them from being used again by the Vietcong. It was after one of these Free Fire Zone incidents that an anonymous American officer was reported to have said, "We had to destroy the village in order to save it."

With the exception of the Green Berets, few American soldiers and almost no high-ranking officers were trained for jungle warfare during the early years of the war. At one time, in fact, not one of the dozens of generals serving in Vietnam had taken counterinsurgency training at Fort Bragg, North Carolina. Such fighting, however, was a tradition that went back to the beginnings of United States history. The early American colonists had fought the British regulars in guerrilla fashion during the Revolutionary War. And for more than 200 years, from colonial days right up to the last of the Indian wars on the western plains in the nineteenth century, American soldiers had been engaged constantly in antiguerrilla warfare with the North American Indians who were masters of the hit-and-run attack. There had been some small-unit guerrilla action in World War II, but the last major antiguerrilla warfare in which U.S. soldiers had been engaged was in the Philippines during the Spanish-American War near the start of the twentieth century. Since then American soldiers had grown accustomed to fighting conventionally in conventional wars, depending heavily on massive firepower to defeat the enemy.

But in the jungle, against fast-striking Vietcong guerrillas, heavy firepower was of little use. Rifles, grenades, portable mortars, and light machine guns were standard American equipment. In combat the M-1 rifle was not as effective as the Soviet-made AK-47 rifle used by the Vietcong. The M-1 was more prone to jamming and, because of its size and weight, it was not as maneuverable in thick brush as the AK-47. South Vietnamese troops, most of whom were no more than five feet tall and weighed no more than one hundred pounds, had difficulty using the M-1. They preferred the lightweight carbine or M-16, as did many jungle-fighting GIs.

American troops either were fed at their temporary base camps between patrols or carried K and C rations with them while on patrol. The Vietcong—called VC or "Victor Charlies" by the GIs—carried food tubes around their necks containing enough rice to last each man a week.

Not only were most American infantrymen untrained in counterinsurgency warfare, but most of them were also young men of nineteen or twenty who had been drafted into military service and were still civilians at heart. Many of them arrived in Vietnam like tourists, carrying their cameras and transistor radios. An armed forces radio station in Saigon broadcast American programs—mostly of popular music—and early in the war all too many grunts took their transistor radios right into combat with them. Australian troops, most of whom were seasoned veterans, for a time refused to go on joint combat operations with the Americans because often a transistor radio would be playing right in the middle of a firefight. If a grunt had a radio in his pocket, it might be turned off to begin with, but if he had to crawl on his stomach, it could accidentally be turned on and an American pop tune would blare forth in the jungle and reveal the patrol to the enemy.

Among the worst hazards American infantrymen had to face in the jungle were the various booby traps set by the VC. Most common were the *punji* pits. These were camouflaged holes filled with razor-sharp, upright bamboo stakes that could pierce a soldier's feet, legs, groin, and stomach if he stumbled into one of them. *Punji* sticks were also hidden in mud balls left hanging by jungle vines along a trail into which GIs might walk and be wounded.

Dap loi were made from empty .50 caliber machine gun shells that were filled with new powder and chunks of scrap metal and sealed with wax. The refilled shells were then placed in a bamboo cylinder with a nail point at the bottom. The *dap loi* were then buried along a jungle trail so only the wax top was above ground. When stepped on, the shell case was pushed down onto the nail point which activated the gunpowder primer and blew scrap metal into the unwary soldier's foot.

Various other booby traps caused numerous casualties and badly damaged American combat troop morale. They included carefully concealed land mines, grenades triggered by hidden trip wires placed alongside jungle trails or on the banks of streams, and steel-pointed arrows automatically fired by trip wires from bows hidden in the brush.

It seemed little wonder that some American soldiers, faced with jungle warfare day after day, soon lost their traditional attitude of fair play toward the enemy. As one young infantryman put it: "Anything that moves is suspect. Anything that's dead is Vietcong. Men, women, and children. It's all the same thing." This was by no means a general attitude among all American GIs, but it was widespread enough so that later it led to tragic atrocities committed against Vietnamese civilians.

Frustrated by the lack of success against the North Vietnamese in both aerial and guerrilla warfare, General Westmoreland was faced with a new threat in the fall of 1965. This was the possibility of the enemy inflicting a major defeat on Montagnard and Green Beret forces in the Central Highlands near the Cambodian border. There the Vietcong had concentrated a force of some 6,000 men and were threatening to capture the provincial capital of Pleiku and then continue their drive eastward to the China Sea. If the drive was successful, Westmoreland believed, the whole Vietnam peninsula would be cut in half far below the 17th parallel or DMZ.

General Westmoreland regarded the plan as another opportunity to strike a decisive blow against a large, concentrated VC force. The North Vietnamese troops included Vietcong guerrillas and elite members of the regular North Vietnamese Army (AVN), many of whom had been trained in China. Westmoreland countered the threat on Pleiku by airlifting the equally elite U.S. First Cavalry Airmobile Division by helicopter into the combat area, located in the Ia Drang Valley.

The Montagnards and Green Berets were able to hold off the first North Vietnamese attacks which began in mid-November. When the "First Cav" arrived, its members scarcely had time to set up a temporary base camp before the North Vietnamese struck in full force. They attacked for a week virtually without letup but failed to overrun the First Cav defensive position. The Americans and Montagnards were greatly aided by continued air support from fighter-bombers and B-52 strategic bombers. This ground–air support by B-52s marked the first time these huge bombers had been used in a tactical battle situation, and their highly accurate precision bombing was remarkable. Interestingly, it was in this same fashion that the French had wanted the United States to use its B-52s at Dien Bien Phu.

On November 19 the North Vietnamese broke off the battle and retreated. They were badly mauled by First Cav counterattacks all the way to the Cambodian border. The outcome of the battle was heralded as a major victory by General Westmoreland, the Johnson administration, and the American communications media—press, radio, and television. It was announced that 1,800 North Vietnamese had been killed as opposed to 250 American and Montagnard dead. Enthusiastic predictions were made about the future use of highly mobile, "heli-lifted" American combat divisions in major battles throughout Vietnam. But this, of course, would call for additional troop shipments from the United States.

There were at least two drawbacks to the American victory. First of all, several high-ranking American intelligence officers pointed out that the reason North Vietnamese losses were so high in the Ia Drang Valley battle was that the elite AVN and VC troops had been willing to sacrifice lives to test the American firepower methods. What the North Vietnamese had discovered was that if they moved in close enough to American defense positions—perhaps as close as thirty or forty yards—American air and artillery power could be neutralized. The Americans would not risk killing their own men by firing artillery shells or dropping bombs that close to their own positions. This was a costly lesson but a lesson the North Vietnamese learned well in the Ia Drang Valley. They were to use it successfully throughout the rest of the war.

Second, and perhaps more important, was the fact that when the Vietcong and AVN had broken off the battle, they had been far from destroyed as a fighting force. They had simply retreated into Cambodia, where they were reinforced and resupplied, and were soon ready to emerge in full strength into Vietnam. Because Cambodia was a neutral country, the U.S. State Department would not allow American military forces to follow the enemy into Cambodia even in "hot pursuit." The military claimed that the right of hot pursuit was acceptable under international law and did not violate Cambodia's neutrality. It meant chasing the enemy a short distance into Cambodia, provided contact with the enemy was first made in Vietnam.

Cambodia became a privileged sanctuary for North Vietnamese military forces, a situation that was to hamper the U.S. military effort throughout much of the war. An attempt to solve the problem by force during the Nixon administration would also create one of the most controversial and tragic episodes of the Vietnam conflict and its aftermath.

5.

"WINNING THE HEARTS
AND MINDS
OF THE PEOPLE"

The American victory near Pleiku in the Ia Drang Valley and the promise of more encouraged the United States to send more troops to Vietnam. In the spring of 1966 Defense Secretary McNamara announced that American forces in South Vietnam numbered almost 250,000. Before the year was out this number would increase to almost 400,000, and this would not include some 60,000 men in the U.S. fleet and more than 30,000 stationed in Thailand.

But no decisive victories followed. The Search and Destroy missions continued to be carried out on a larger scale than before, and the Free Fire Zone technique continued to disrupt the lives of the Vietnamese villagers—if it accomplished nothing else. The aerial bombing of North Vietnam as well as Vietcong-held territory below the DMZ increased. During these bombings many Vietnamese civilians were killed, and when asked if this aspect of the war, especially in South Vietnam, did not bother him, General Westmoreland told a newspaper correspondent, "Yes, but it does deprive the enemy of the population, doesn't it?"

Nothing that the Americans did seemed to put a stop to the flow of North Vietnamese infiltrators down the 1,000-mile-long Ho Chi Minh Trail into South Vietnam. In fact, the number grew from 1,500 men a month at the start of the war to almost 9,000 a month at the end of 1966. Now they came in platoons and companies that reformed into regiments and divisions below the DMZ.

In a desperate attempt to stop the Vietcong from moving south, Defense Secretary McNamara came up with a fanciful idea for detecting all such infiltrators automatically. This was an electronic fence or barrier that would stretch across Vietnam slightly below the DMZ. McNamara actually put several Harvard scientists to work on the project at a cost of half a million dollars in Defense Department funds before it was abandoned as impractical. First of all, as many as half a dozen divisions of army engineers would have been needed to construct such an electronic marvel, and then additional thousands of troops would have had to man the various fortified strongpoints along "McNamara's Line."

What McNamara was reaching for—in fact what most of the American civilian and military planners were reaching for—was some way to bring to bear on the conflict the full weight of the nation's scientific, technological, industrial, and military might. What they did not fully realize until it was too late was that the Vietnam War was more a political conflict than it was a military one, and as such it would be won or lost in the hearts and minds of the men and women involved on both sides.

From the beginning various American and South Vietnamese leaders had tried a series of so-called "pacification programs" in order to win "the hearts and minds of the people." Basically these programs were aimed at weaning the Vietnamese away from communism and toward democracy. But as American military strength increased in South Vietnam, the various pacification programs were dropped so that the United States could get on with winning the war militarily.

The pacification programs were designed to improve the life of the Vietnamese people in rural areas, both economically and politically. Roads, bridges, and canals were rebuilt, and modern agricultural methods were introduced. These changes were financed with American funds and supervised by American technical advisers. The democratic election of local village officials was also encouraged.

In order to carry out the programs in the rural countryside, an attempt was made to fortify certain centrally located villages against attack by the Vietcong. People from nearby unprotected villages would then be moved to the fortified villages. There they would be protected from the Vietcong and reeducated regarding the evils of communism and the benefits of democracy. This was called the "Strategic Hamlet" program.

The program failed for two basic reasons. The villagers resented being uprooted from their ancestral homes and resettled in what many regarded as concentration camps, where they had to spend much of their time building fortifications. In addition, the Vietcong simply could not be kept from infiltrating even the Strategic Hamlets. At least one American adviser insisted that whenever the lights were turned out for the showing of an educational film to the gathered villagers, members of the Vietcong quietly crept in and joined the audience.

"I knew most of the VC, like the rest of the audience, had never seen movies before, and they wanted to see one," the adviser said. "And dressed in those pajama-like clothes they all wore, everybody looked alike."

All pacification programs were dealt a severe blow when several successive South Vietnamese presidents beginning with Diem refused to hold general elections and continued their dictatorial reigns. They were further damaged by the resettlement of the populations of whole villages caused by the Strategic Hamlet program, as well as by the Free Fire Zone campaigns. To the Vietnamese people, their ancestors—and the local villages in which they and their ancestors before them had lived—were sacred. When the villagers were uprooted, their lives in a very real sense were destroyed. "The laws of the emperor are less important than the customs of the village" was an old Vietnamese saying. Americans tended not to understand or sympathize with this attitude.

Among American combat troops this lack of sympathy was dramatically displayed when so-called "Zippo Brigades" used their cigarette lighters to set fire to thatched villages suspected of hiding members of the Vietcong. Such callous acts partially explained why so many villagers were Vietcong sympathizers. They were inclined to regard U.S. soldiers simply as successors to the hated French, and to accept the VC as liberating heroes.

Most rural villagers did not have the faintest idea of what either communism or democracy was, but they could tell the difference between Vietcong and American soldiers by their actions, and all things considered they often preferred the VC. VC soldiers, for example, might take over a village, and this the villagers did not especially like. But often the VC helped farmers with their work and cared for the ill and needy. Green Beret teams included paramedics who were trained to improve the health of rural populations, but the Green Berets were relatively few in number. The doctors and medics with regular U.S. combat troops were inclined to look after the American sick and wounded first and Vietnamese civilians second, if at all.

Nevertheless, the Vietcong did hide in Vietnamese villages, and flushing them out was always a difficult and dangerous job. Rookie U.S. troops entering a village might find nothing but old men, women, and children. Perhaps there would be a handful of primitive tools lying about, and in the thatched huts there would be only cooking pots, stone jars filled with rice, and sleeping mats. Mats usually covered root cellars as well. It would be altogether an innocent-looking scene.

But veteran grunts learned to probe dirt floors with their bayonets and to inspect root cellars thoroughly. Often they found the opening to a tunnel or a series of tunnels that led into the jungle, or even to another village. These tunnels were small, just large enough to give the slightly built Vietcong crawl space but not large enough to admit a GI. When they were dug up, they often were found to contain storerooms filled with food, land mines, ammunition, grenades, small arms—everything needed to resupply a guerrilla force working in the neighborhood.

So many of these tunnels and their secret storerooms were discovered that some American combat troops claimed that there was just one vast, mole-like system of underground passageways beneath the surface of the whole country. After the first few tunnel openings were discovered, American troops became more and more ruthless in their sweeps through suspect villages.

In fact, as the war progressed and the fighting became

more severe, American military forces were accused of destroying whoever and whatever was in their path, including civilians and even cultural shrines. Antiwar critics said that American soldiers seemed to think that freedom for the Vietnamese simply meant freedom from Ho Chi Minh and communism, and nothing more. The United States, these critics added, was prepared to destroy not just an occasional village but the whole of Vietnam "in order to save it."

Certainly some of this criticism was justified. The slaughter of innocent women and children at the village of My Lai in 1968 was barbaric and indefensible. There were other similar tragic incidents, but fortunately they were few and isolated. Unfortunately, their perpetrators were not always dealt with promptly. A serious effort, for example, was made to cover up the My Lai atrocity.

The destruction of national shrines also occurred. During the massive Vietcong Tet offensive, also in 1968, the city of Hue, which was the nation's cultural capital, was virtually destroyed by U.S. bombs, napalm, and gunfire. Other less well-known shrines were also severely damaged during the course of the war. Critics said that this sort of thing had not happened in Europe during World War II because the Americans were racists who respected Europeans and European cultural centers, while they neither understood nor respected Asians or their cultural monuments. This accusation was partially but not wholly true.

It was true that before the invasion of France in 1944 General Eisenhower had warned his commanders and their troops against inflicting casualties on French civilians and damaging "historical monuments and cultural centers which symbolize to the world all that we are fighting to preserve." Eisenhower's orders had been followed, but mainly because the French population as a whole was on the side of the Allies. In addition, the Germans had allowed Paris to become an open city and did not try to defend it.

Earlier in World War II a world-famous Benedictine monastery in Italy, Monte Cassino, had been bombed and severely damaged by American forces under General Mark Clark. The excuse was that Monte Cassino was being used by German observers who could call down artillery fire on advancing U.S. troops. After the war General Clark said the bombing was a mistake, but at the time it had seemed necessary.

Monte Cassino was not an isolated incident. Numerous other European shrines and cultural centers had been dealt with ruthlessly by both sides in World War II, and countless civilians had been killed in the process. The truth of the matter is that in war, and most especially in modern total war, whole populations and their works are subject to destruction, and certainly the Vietnamese were no exception. A more basic question, perhaps, is whether or not the United States had any business being in Vietnam in the first place. Certainly many Vietnamese and particularly the North Vietnamese and their National Liberation Front (NLF) did not think so.

The NLF was the political arm of the Vietcong. To understand what made the Vietcong such a fierce and stubborn foe, it is important to realize that all Vietcong military commanders were responsible to the NLF political leaders. Thus in the North Vietnamese armed forces, politics and the military effort were inseparable. But politics to the NLF meant much more than it normally means in the Western world. Politics to the NLF was virtually a form of religion, a religion dedicated to the independence and freedom of Vietnam from interference by all foreign nations.

In this sense the NLF and Vietcong were not unlike Sam Adams and his fellow "Sons of Liberty" in the American Colonies, who preached independence from Great Britain and were also willing to risk their lives to obtain it. In events like the Boston Tea Party, when Sam Adams and his "Indians" boarded British ships in Boston harbor and threw chests of tea overboard to protest British taxes, politics and acts of violence often become intermixed and indistinguishable. Frequently, if a cause burns brightly enough in the hearts and minds of a people, political beliefs turn them into fanatical zealots who are willing to risk all—their "lives, their fortunes, and their sacred honor." And so it was with the NLF and the Vietcong, but American leaders could not or would not believe that communism could inspire such loyalty.

In clinging to the idea of communism's inevitable failure and democracy's invincibility, America's leaders failed to win the hearts and minds of the Vietnamese. But more importantly, they failed to win the hearts and minds of the American public—especially the nation's young people. This was made crystal clear when student antiwar demonstrations began to break out across the United States.

Americans who favored the nation's involvement in Vietnam were called "Hawks." Those who opposed it were called "Doves." Since the start of the conflict there had been a sizable antiwar movement, but beginning in 1965 more and more young people joined the ranks of the Doves. This was especially true on college and university campuses.

In mid-October of 1965 a national "Weekend of Protest" was held during which there was a large parade for peace in New York and major student demonstrations in California, Wisconsin, and Washington, D.C. In New York twenty-two-year-old David J. Miller became the first person to burn his draft registration card publicly. He was later arrested. Despite Miller's arrest and a federal law that made draft card destruction a criminal offense, many young people continued to defy the law by publicly burning their cards.

In Washington a young Quaker, Norman Morrison, went one step further and staged the ultimate protest by burning himself to death. Also in the nation's capital, some 20,000 protestors paraded before the White House chanting: "Hey! Hey! LBJ! How many kids did you kill today?"

Members of the White House staff later reported that President Lyndon B. Johnson suffered more over this taunt than he did over any other incident during the war. Johnson had started his political career in Texas as an administrator in one of President Franklin D. Roosevelt's youth programs during the economic Depression of the 1930s, and he continued to think that the future of the country lay in its young people. Even when antiwar demonstrators picketed LBJ's Texas ranch demanding that the bombing in Vietnam be stopped, Johnson steadfastly maintained that the young people's dissent grew out of their ignorance. "They wouldn't know a Communist," he said, "if they tripped over one."

Many Hawks accused the Dove demonstrators of being disloyal to the United States. But the days of Senator

Joseph McCarthy's Red-baiting were over, and many prominent national figures joined the growing antiwar movement during the next several years. Among them were actress Jane Fonda, singer Joan Baez, pediatrician Dr. Benjamin Spock, cartoonist Jules Feiffer, writer Saul Bellow, sculptor Alexander Calder, and numerous others.

The youthful Doves were not purely idealistic, of course. Many simply did not want to be drafted. When the war began, most college students were deferred from the draft if they maintained good grades. Some Dove professors aided students by giving them higher marks than they deserved. This practice became so widespread that after the war prospective employers often automatically lowered by a full grade point the marks of wartime graduates seeking postwar jobs—from an A to a B, for example. It also caused postwar reevaluations of grading practices on college and university campuses.

The blanket deferment of college students also led to the justifiable complaint by those who could not afford to go to college that the Vietnam conflict was "a rich man's war and a poor man's fight." As the war escalated, however, blanket deferments began to be eliminated. In 1965 draft calls averaged 5,000 men a month. In 1966 they increased to 50,000 a month, an average that was fairly steadily maintained until Richard Nixon became president. Nixon had always believed that the draft was the main reason for the widespread protest movement. But he failed to prove his point when draft calls were sharply reduced and troop withdrawals from Vietnam were begun in 1969. On November 15 of that year some 250,000 demonstrators gathered in Washington in the largest antiwar protest in U.S. history.

Draft Director General Lewis Hershey also added to the military manpower pool early in the war when he ordered that all young antiwar demonstrators be reclassified as 1-A and be made eligible for the draft immediately. The American Civil Liberties Union protested this police-power use of the draft, but to no avail. Following the lifting of blanket deferments for students and General Hershey's decree, other methods of draft evasion became widespread. These included flunking physical examinations by taking drugs, joining religious cults and declaring conscientious objector status, and simply leaving the country.

Canada and Sweden were the two favorite sanctuaries chosen by draft-evading Americans, and by 1967 there were some 15,000 young American expatriates making new homes in Toronto and Stockholm. They were joined by several thousand deserters from the United States armed services. Military desertions grew as the number of those killed, wounded, and missing in Vietnam increased from 2,500 in 1965, to 33,000 in 1966, to 80,000 in 1967, and to 130,000 in 1968. U.S. casualties in the Korean War had totalled about 34,000 killed and 103,000 wounded.

Despite growing civilian dissent and without American military success that might justify the growing number of casualties, the United States government gave no indication that it was even considering withdrawing from Vietnam. In fact, various U.S. leaders insisted that the conflict could be won in 1967—or by 1968 at the very latest. Like some great runaway machine, the war seemed to have taken off on its own.

6.
BODY COUNTS
AND KILL RATIOS

By 1967 the Vietcong had 25 divisions or about 300,000 troops in South Vietnam. They were, of course, supported by an unestimated number of Vietcong sympathizers among the civilian population, many of whom also played part-time guerrilla roles. Before the year was out there would be almost half a million American troops —more than in the Korean War at its peak—opposing the Vietcong. Supporting the Americans were several hundred thousand ARVN troops plus an estimated 300,-000 members of the South Vietnamese militia. This latter police-type force was supposed to protect local villages or hamlets, which it seldom succeeded in doing. Support of American troops by the ARVN forces was also a somewhat questionable matter. Although there was heavy fighting in 1967, at least one ARVN division lost more men in traffic accidents than it did in combat. In addition, ARVN troops often failed in the task they were frequently assigned—occupying and holding territory once it was captured.

In escalating the war in response to General Westmoreland's never-ending demands for more troops, the

Johnson administration continued to seek a South Vietnamese president who could stabilize his country and gain popular support for his regime. The United States had hopefully supported the several presidents who had succeeded Diem in office, but each had been a disappointment. Consequently, U.S. officials had also supported the overthrow of each successive South Vietnamese presidential failure. As historian Stephen Ambrose pointed out, "Like the owners of an American baseball team, they decided to fire the manager while retaining the team."

Now, however, the Johnson administration was sure it had the right president in the person of General Nguyen Van Thieu. Thieu, who was one of the generals who had led the coup against Diem, was believed to have wide popular support. He was elected president in September of 1967 and would serve in that role for the rest of the war. In an attempt to preserve some sort of executive continuity, Nguyen Cao Ky, who had preceded Thieu as president, was chosen to serve as his vice-president. Air Force Commander Ky was especially popular with the Americans because he was a violent anticommunist.

Twice during the year President Johnson called General Westmoreland back to the United States to bolster the war effort by explaining to the nation what was happening in Vietnam. In April Westmoreland spoke at an Associated Press dinner in New York at which he was optimistic about the outcome of the war and critical of demonstrators who burned the American flag and otherwise encouraged the enemy. This speech angered the antiwar critics who accused both Westmoreland and President Johnson of false patriotism. Later, some 35,-

000 of these critics demonstrated before the Pentagon in Washington.

In November Westmoreland again returned to Washington and spoke on several national television programs as well as before the National Press Club. This time he was more optimistic than ever, and he had apparent reason to be. Between early January and mid-May Westmoreland had launched two of the largest American-ARVN attacks of the war. The first was called "Operation Cedar Falls" and involved some 30,000 American-led troops. The area attacked was known as the "Iron Triangle," located just twenty miles north of Saigon. The Iron Triangle had been a Vietcong headquarters area since the war with the French. In three weeks the entire area had been cleared of Vietcong troops and their sympathizers.

The second attack, "Operation Junction City," involved some 45,000 American and ARVN troops. It was launched against another VC headquarters in the jungle area near the Cambodian border. This battle had lasted for twelve weeks and had ended with the Vietcong in full retreat into Cambodia.

"I have never been more encouraged since I have been in Vietnam," Westmoreland told his Washington audience. Then he added, in words that were to come back to haunt him: "We have reached an important point when the end begins to come into view." He predicted that within the foreseeable future the withdrawal of American troops could begin—if, of course, he was first given the necessary number of additional troops to finish the war.

Perhaps unfortunately, many Americans did not seem

to be impressed by Westmoreland's optimism. Newspapermen caustically called his National Press Club talk "The Light at the End of the Tunnel" speech, and several congressmen were equally skeptical. Among the latter was Senator George Aiken of Vermont, who earlier had suggested that the government should "simply announce that the United States has won the war and then withdraw its troops from Vietnam." Aiken said he still thought this was an excellent idea.

Westmoreland returned to Vietnam well aware that his additional troop demands had fallen on virtually deaf ears in Washington. In fact, President Johnson had established a troop ceiling of 525,000 men, the number that could be sent without calling up active military reserves—an act that Johnson shied away from as political suicide in view of the upcoming national elections. Johnson was still determined to get more of his Great Society measures passed as well as win the war. His political hero, Franklin Roosevelt, had been successful in pushing through Congress his New Deal measures as well as in leading the nation to victory in World War II. But Johnson was forgetting, or choosing to ignore, that FDR had not tried to do both at the same time. Nor had FDR tried to carry on a prolonged conflict without a declaration of war by Congress.

Numerous congressmen were now pointing this out to Johnson and openly criticizing him in other ways. Even members of his own party, the Democrats, were saying that if FDR had lived the United States would never have become involved in Indochina, which is probably true. Toward the end of World War II, FDR had said on numerous occasions that the peace settlement should include provisions against France's reestablishing its foreign colonies in both Africa and Indochina.

What Westmoreland had not told his Washington audiences was that Operation Cedar Falls had indeed cleared the Iron Triangle of the enemy, but a week after the operation ended the Vietcong were once again active in the area. After Operation Junction City it took the VC somewhat longer to return, but within six months they were back in force. In addition, in both operations thousands of civilian Vietnamese had been forced to flee into Saigon because of the Free Fire Zone tactics used by Westmoreland's forces. From the Iron Triangle area alone, where dozens of villages were destroyed and many miles of tunnels were dug up by bulldozers, almost 10,000 refugees fled into the South Vietnamese capital. This strained to the breaking point the capital's already critical supply situation. Herbicides to destroy the jungle cover were also used in both operations, making an area the size of Massachusetts uninhabitable except by combat troops.

Because of aerial saturation bombing, the Vietcong suffered many more casualties than the American-ARVN forces, and Westmoreland pointed to this "body count" of the enemy dead as another indication of victory. But body counts alone meant little if conquered ground could not be occupied and held. As historian Frances FitzGerald has pointed out, "The commanding general never quite came to terms with the fact that the war was being fought at points rather than along lines." Furthermore, there were soon reasons to believe that most body-count statistics were false.

When both the American and ARVN combat troops

learned that command headquarters was judging the success or failure of an operation by the number of enemy dead reported, body count figures immediately began to soar. Some of these figures were simply made up, and most included dead civilian men, women, and children. Not infrequently the number of destroyed thatched huts in a village would be counted and their number multiplied by an estimate of how many people they had probably contained. ARVN troops especially were bewildered by this curious way of running a war, but if the Americans wanted body counts, then body counts they would get—and in abundance. The U.S. military command also played games with the enemy Order of Battle, or the actual number of enemy combat troops. The U.S. Central Intelligence Agency (CIA) consistently (and secretly) reported the number of Vietcong and North Vietnamese troops as between 500,000 and 600,000. This was several hundred thousand more of the enemy than the Pentagon wanted to be made public. Consequently, the North Vietnamese and Vietcong Order of Battle was officially said to total 300,000 men —or less. This manipulation of numbers was supposed to prevent the public from being frightened and, as the conflict continued, the total dropped below 300,000, to prove that the United States and South Vietnam were winning the war.

Nevertheless, because of the American-ARVN "victories" in the Iron Triangle and near the Cambodian border, Westmoreland ordered similar offensive operations in the Mekong Delta region as well as in the Central Highlands area near the border of Laos and just below the DMZ. Once again great successes were reported, especially in the Central Highlands campaign which began in March and lasted most of the rest of the year. The enemy body count was enormous at such places as Con Thien and Khe Sanh and especially at Dak To. But once again no territory remained under American-ARVN control, and thousands of additional civilian refugees fled the area.

Below the DMZ an attempt was made to house 20,000 of the refugees in hastily built army barracks, but little or no provisions were made to feed them. The great success of the jungle defoliation campaign was matched by the successful destruction of the rice crop. Westmoreland's command justified this so-called "resources control program" by pointing out that it denied food to the enemy. But it was usually the civilians who suffered, since the VC combat troops carried their food with them or could be supplied by porters with their cargo bicycles.

The fighting at Dak To was the heaviest in the Highlands since that in the Ia Drang Valley in 1966. When it ended late in 1967 the enemy had left behind some 1,400 dead—a "kill ratio" Westmoreland's headquarters proudly proclaimed to be 10 to 1 in favor of the Americans. Despite such favorable body counts and kill ratios, an ominous note began to be sounded by American intelligence officers as the year drew to a close. The Vietcong were apparently preparing for a major offensive somewhere in South Vietnam. VC troop reinforcements were flooding down the Ho Chi Minh Trail, and enemy plans captured at Dak To seemed to confirm suspicions of some sort of large-scale enemy assault.

Just before Christmas Westmoreland cabled his suspicions to Washington, and if they failed to disturb the Joint Chiefs of Staff they more than succeeded in disturbing President Johnson. "We don't want one of them 'Din

Bin Phoos'," he told his aides. The fighting at Con Thien earlier in the year had for a time developed siege qualities, and newspaper correspondents had taken to referring to the battle there as "an American Dien Bien Phu." Now Westmoreland reported that the VC had massed several fresh divisions before Khe Sanh. Perhaps an American Dien Bien Phu was to take place there.

Johnson sought reassurance from the Joint Chiefs, who told him that any such offensive could be contained quickly and that it might even be a good thing if it happened. That way the bulk of Giap's forces could be faced in a set piece battle and destroyed. Consequently, no attempt was made either by Westmoreland or Johnson to alert the media and the American public to the possibility of any major VC offensive. There was even some doubt as to whether such a warning would have been believed, since just a short time earlier Westmoreland had assured the nation that the end of the war had begun to come into view.

In any event, the light at the end of the tunnel was just about to go out.

The old Imperial capital and cultural center of Hue during the Tet offensive. *Defense Department Photos*

This key North Vietnamese bridge was destroyed by U.S. aerial attacks.
Defense Department Photo

Two Vietcong guerrillas.
UPI Photo

ARVN troops wade through the mud to board a U.S. Navy patrol boat.
U.S. Navy Photo

Army choppers land in a jungle clearing. *U.S. Army Photo*

A B-52 Stratafortress drops bombs over North Vietnam. *U.S. Air Force Photo*

(LEFT) Outside a Saigon orphanage, Master Sergeant Bobbie Loeschner, Sr., holds the Vietnamese child he rescued from a destroyed village and later adopted. *Courtesy of Bobbie Loeschner, Sr.* (RIGHT) In the late 1970s Bobbie Loeschner, Jr., attended high school in the Midwest and excelled in baseball. *Courtesy of Ethel Daccardo*

Six years after he was captured by the North Vietnamese, Major Floyd Kushner was released and returned to the United States in 1973. The former POW is shown with his family after his arrival at Valley Forge Hospital, Pennsylvania. This was the first time Major Kushner had seen his son. *UPI Photo*

A sick old Vietnamese man is carried to safety by a U.S. marine from a village that had been infiltrated by the Vietcong. *UPI Photo*

This Vietnamese mother and her children had to escape across a river near their village when the village was bombed by U.S. planes. *UPI Photo*

Terrified Vietnamese children attempt to escape after an American aerial napalm strike in South Vietnam. The girl in the center of this prize-winning photograph has torn off her burning clothes. *Wide World Photos*

A Vietnamese boy carries his dog and small sack of food as he leaves his home village after the allied attack on the Vietcong stronghold in the Iron Triangle north of Saigon. *Wide World Photos*

Vietnamese peasants flee from their village during an American "search and destroy" mission. *Wide World Photos*

7.
THE TET OFFENSIVE

The Vietnamese traditionally measure the year, not by the Western calendar, but by cycles of the moon. This is called "the lunar year." The beginning of the lunar year is celebrated by a holiday called *Tet.* Tet is a combination New Year's Eve celebration and period of religious worship. It lasts for several days and is observed by almost all Vietnamese. There are fireworks displays, parades, street festivals, and widespread worship at family shrines. Historically, even wars were usually halted during Tet, and it was assumed by both the North and South Vietnamese as well as the Americans that this would be the case at the start of the Tet holiday on January 30, 1968.

But Ho Chi Minh was an excellent student of history. He recalled that back in the late eighteenth century when the Chinese had captured and occupied Hanoi, the Vietnamese had launched a surprise attack against the Chinese and driven them out of the city. That attack had been a surprise because it was launched during a Tet "truce." Why shouldn't the same deception work again?

Publicly, Ho Chi Minh agreed to a Tet truce to last

from January 27 to February 3, 1968. Privately, he ordered General Giap to prepare his VC forces to strike on January 30. So that Giap's troops could continue their buildup unhampered by air raids, Ho Chi Minh also announced that if U.S. bombing was stopped he would agree to peace talks. The United States agreed.

One of General Giap's favorite stories was the ancient legend about the Greek warriors besieging Troy who had built a huge, hollow wooden horse and then hid inside it. When the curious Trojans threw open the gates of Troy and hauled the horse inside the city's walls, the Greek warriors entered the city too. They waited until nightfall and then emerged from the horse to kill the sleeping Trojans and set fire to the city. Giap had no intention of concealing any of his VC warriors inside a wooden horse—Americans might know that historic trick —but there were certainly numerous wooden coffins moving through the streets of South Vietnamese cities that could well conceal weapons and ammunition, if not men.

If South Vietnamese city dwellers and their American allies were aware of the amazing increase in the number of funerals held in their cities during the several weeks before Tet, they put it down perhaps to the growing number of war casualties. What was more difficult to explain, however, was that most funeral processions were almost wholly made up of husky young men of military age. These grim young strangers spoke to no one and had eyes only for the wooden coffins they guarded with seemingly fierce dedication. The South Vietnamese civilians and the Americans could, of course, be forgiven if they assumed that the deadly contents of these coffins were merely corpses.

They learned otherwise early on the morning of January 30 when the Vietcong suddenly struck at more than one hundred cities—provincial and district capitals throughout South Vietnam. In Saigon itself VC guerrillas, armed with weapons from their secret coffin caches, blasted their way into the American embassy compound, killing several U.S. Marines. Elsewhere throughout the city, VC forces fought their way into the grounds of the Presidential Palace, captured a government radio station, and blew up aircraft at a nearby airfield.

In the Mekong Delta, the most populous and supposedly most secure area in South Vietnam, the VC surprised ARVN forces and took over several headquarters. Elsewhere, a huge American base at Cam Ranh Bay and the ARVN military academy and resort area for army officers at Da Lat also came under heavy attack by half a dozen VC battalions. Simultaneously, other VC battalions besieged the important American airfield at Da Nang, destroying dozens of planes and thus preventing immediate aerial counterattacks. At Khe Sanh some 20,-000 Vietcong and North Vietnamese regulars surrounded 10,000 U.S. Marines, and then additional VC battalions swung around the powerless Khe Sanh forces to strike at Hue. There they easily overcame the skeleton force of ARVN defense troops and soon took over most of the ancient cultural capital.

Although they had had some warning of the impending attacks, General Westmoreland and his Allied command were almost completely surprised by their timing and widespread nature. Most ARVN forces were away from their units observing the Tet holiday, and American units were not on an attack-alert status. In Saigon only a few hundred U.S. soldiers were immediately available to fend off the VC forces, but they did manage to retake the American embassy within a few hours. During the first day helicopter gunships were called into action. They drove the VC from the radio station by destroying the entire building along with several hundred precious —at least to the GIs—rock music recordings and tapes. The grounds of the Presidential Palace were also successfully retaken.

Elsewhere throughout the city fierce fighting and sniper activity continued for days, even after major reinforcements arrived. Tanks were used to try to dislodge the VC from buildings they had occupied, and numerous fire fights took place in marketplaces within sight and sound of the American embassy. Soldiers working at army headquarters in Saigon—"Headquarters Commandos," they called themselves—suddenly discovered they had become front line troops and desperately tried to recall their basic training combat lessons. Fires raged unchecked for a week, and thousands of civilians fled the city on foot or on bicycles or tricycles, carrying their dead and wounded with them and seriously obstructing Allied troop movements. Adding to the panic were the wild rumors that many Vietcong guerrillas were wearing captured ARVN uniforms.

Since Saigon was the headquarters for numerous journalists and television crews, the American public was almost immediately made aware of much of the chaos created by the VC attack. People sitting in their living rooms in the United States soon were seeing scenes of wartime horror half a world away in a city they had been told was virtually free from enemy action. What had happened in this war the United States was supposed to be winning? If the fire fights had been taking place in Hanoi, that would make sense. But in Saigon, the capital of South Vietnam and headquarters of the American war effort? That made no sense at all. America's doubts and wonderings were to continue and grow during the next several weeks as news of the Vietcong Tet offensive elsewhere in Vietnam gradually became known.

Within a matter of days after the offensive began, the Vietcong controlled large areas of the countryside as well as numerous provincial and district capitals. Since his forces had never had any major permanent success in countryside campaigns, General Westmoreland now concentrated his command's efforts in retaking the large population centers.

At Da Lat the VC took control of the central marketplace where they set up fortifications and withstood counterattacks for several weeks. At Ben Tre the VC also stubbornly fought off weeks of counterattack. When these two provincial capitals were finally overrun there was little left to retake. They too had been "destroyed in order to be saved."

Having begun shortly before the Tet offensive actually got under way, the siege of the U.S. Marine forces at Khe Sanh was to last for seventy-seven days. Situated in a natural amphitheater circled by clay hills, Khe Sanh was similar geographically to Dien Bien Phu. Since it was also on a major route along which VC reinforcements moved southward, it was a key strongpoint in the American defense of South Vietnam. One of the reasons Khe Sanh was so stoutly defended, according to Westmoreland's command, was that it was "like the cork in a bottle. Once the VC pull that cork they can get by us there and take over the whole countryside to the south."

But once the marines were surrounded by the enemy,

the VC made no serious effort to capture Khe Sanh. They simply bypassed it with part of their forces while additional forces laid siege to the city and its marine base and steadily lobbed artillery shells into the midst of its beleaguered defenders. This tactic naturally kept thousands of crack U.S. combat troops from fighting elsewhere.

As if to confirm President Johnson's worst fears, media stories once again began to refer to Khe Sanh as "the American Dien Bien Phu." These stories finally ended when a force of 30,000 American troops advanced on Khe Sanh in "Operation Pegasus" and broke the siege. Ironically, a few weeks after the siege was lifted all of the American troops were simply pulled out of Khe Sanh— much to the bewilderment of the marines who had fought so valiantly to defend it.

But the most savage battle was waged for historic Hue. Before it was over—after four long weeks—about 75 percent of the city lay in ruins. Together, Khe Sanh and Hue had the unenviable distinction of being the most heavily bombed targets in military history. ARVN forces first attempted to retake Hue from the Vietcong with little or no success. Westmoreland then ordered in U.S. Marines who fought a bloody house-to-house, street-by-street battle for several weeks. Air strikes were also ordered, and these destroyed many ancient architectural monuments that dated back to Vietnam's precolonial days.

The number of civilian deaths at Hue was huge, as it was throughout South Vietnam during the Tet offensive and the American-ARVN counterattacks. The Allied command estimated there was a total of 165,000 civilians killed throughout South Vietnam, with 2 million more forced to become refugees. Allied military casualties were reported as 4,200 killed and 16,000 wounded. This included both the American and ARVN forces. Vietcong casualties were estimated at 45,000 killed, 100,000 wounded, and 7,000 prisoners of war.

Mainly because of the favorable Allied kill ratio and body count over the VC, Westmoreland's headquarters declared that the Tet offensive was a major defeat for North Vietnam. President Johnson had not waited for the Westmoreland announcement. Two days after the Tet offensive started, Johnson told a press conference that the United States had known all about it ahead of time and that it was a complete failure. Defense Secretary McNamara told a TV audience that, "It's quite clear that the enemy's military objective has not been achieved."

Vermont's crusty Senator Aiken countered with, "If this is failure, I hope the Vietcong never have a major success." And Senator Eugene McCarthy of Minnesota, who planned to oppose Johnson in the forthcoming presidential primary race, said, "If capturing a section of the American embassy and several large cities consti- tutes complete failure, I suppose by this logic that if the Vietcong captured the entire country, the administration would be claiming their total collapse."

Nevertheless, both the Johnson administration and Westmoreland's military command went on claiming vic- tory, apparently unaware of the fact that they had lost the trust of the American public. If the Vietcong had failed to achieve a total military victory, they had certainly suc- ceeded in creating a credibility gap between what Ameri- can leaders said was happening and what actually was happening in Vietnam. Quite simply, few people thought they could believe either President Johnson or General Westmoreland any more.

In many ways the Tet offensive was as important historically as the North Vietnamese victory at Dien Bien Phu. While it did not immediately drive the United States out of the war, it would eventually do so. And almost immediately it drove American political and military leaders out of office and command.

The first to go was Secretary of Defense Robert S. McNamara. He formally left office in February of 1968, although several months earlier President Johnson had announced that McNamara was leaving the Department of Defense to become Director of the World Bank. He was replaced by Clark M. Clifford. At the end of March President Johnson made a surprise announcement regarding his own future plans. He said that he would not seek renomination as the Democratic candidate for the presidency. And in June General Westmoreland was replaced by his deputy commander, General Creighton W. Abrams.

McNamara had gradually shifted his position from that of Hawk to Dove during the course of the war. In the beginning he had been a strong advocate of the American commitment in Vietnam. Soon he had begun to realize, however, that neither aerial bombardment nor additional American troops accomplished anything except to increase North Vietnamese resistance and sink the United States deeper and deeper into the Vietnam quagmire.

To some degree McNamara managed to scale down Westmoreland's troop demands, and he finally openly opposed President Johnson's escalation of the aerial bombing campaign. As McNamara became skeptical about the war, the president sought his advice less and less, and made caustic comments about how the Defense Secretary was disloyally creating a "divided house" in American government. Johnson also began to lean more and more heavily on the advice of Secretary of State Dean Rusk, who was a confirmed Hawk and unwavering anticommunist.

McNamara, as well as President Johnson, was the target of much abuse from antiwar demonstrators in the United States. Among the North Vietnamese he, Rusk, and Johnson were considered the three American war criminals mainly responsible for continuing and escalating the conflict. In 1965 while McNamara was on a fact-finding mission to South Vietnam, a Saigon teenager named Nguyen Van Troi tried to shoot McNamara. The youth was captured, tried, and executed for the assassination attempt. Almost immediately Nguyen Van Troi became a hero in Hanoi, and he and Norman Morrison, the American Quaker who had burned himself to death before the Pentagon, were virtually worshipped throughout North Vietnam as young men who had sacrificed their lives in desperate acts of protest against American involvement in the war.

As the war and McNamara's doubts about its legitimacy both escalated, the Secretary of Defense undertook an unprecedented action in 1967. He ordered a number of research experts to make an exhaustive and honest study of all of the government's classified files on the Vietnam War and the events leading up to it. When the study was finished and McNamara had read it, he was reported by David Halberstam to have said to a friend,

"You know, they could hang people for what's in there."

This study, which was classified as Top Secret, later gained fame as the "Pentagon Papers" when it was leaked to the *New York Times* and other newspapers in June of 1971, during the Nixon administration. An attempt was made by Nixon and his Attorney General, John Mitchell, to suppress publication of the Pentagon Papers, but the U.S. Supreme Court refused to uphold a temporary restraining order.

The forty-seven-volume Pentagon Papers related in some two and a half million words the whole tragic history of the United States' involvement in Vietnam, from the end of World War II through the Johnson administration. The papers clearly showed how the American government under Presidents Truman, Eisenhower, Kennedy, and Johnson had first fully committed the United States—partially because of misguided anticommunist idealism—to intervention in Indochina. They then detailed how each succeeding administration had involved the United States more and more deeply in the Vietnam War itself than was realized at the time by the American public. Perhaps most damning was the disclosure of the Johnson administration's plans to wage war openly against North Vietnam a full year before those plans were made public. One of the documents also revealed that Johnson had his staff prepare a draft of the Tonkin Gulf Resolution even before the Tonkin Gulf incident occurred. The papers also showed that Johnson had told newsmen he had no plans to send troops into action in Vietnam, on the very day that he had decided to do so. In addition, the Pentagon Papers disclosed that intelligence reports consistently indicated that bombing North Vietnam would neither cause Hanoi to stop supporting the Vietcong nor bring Ho Chi Minh to the peace table, yet the bombing had been continued.

The Pentagon Papers were turned over to the *New York Times* by Daniel Ellsberg, one of the people who had worked on them. Ellsberg, who like McNamara had started out as a Hawk but gradually became a Dove, made the papers public because he believed the United States was to blame for the Vietnam tragedy. "There has never been a year when there would have been a war in Indochina without American money," he said. As a responsible American citizen he felt he "could no longer cooperate in concealing this information from the American people. I took this action on my own initiative," Ellsberg concluded, "and I am prepared for all the consequences."

The immediate consequences were quick in coming, but final results were delayed. Ellsberg was arrested in June 1971 and indicted for violating the U.S. Espionage Act. Released on bail, Ellsberg was acquitted of all charges of espionage, theft, and conspiracy in May 1973, after an eighty-nine-day trial.

In 1968 the Pentagon Papers were just being compiled, and President Johnson had no knowledge of the project when he made his surprise announcement about declining to run again for the presidency. Johnson's decision was apparently prompted by America's growing disenchantment with the Vietnam War and his own discouragement about not being able to gain a victory there or with his Great Society legislation.

The immediate incidents that caused Johnson to make his decision not to run began with the presidential primary election in New Hampshire in the spring of 1968. Senator Eugene McCarthy, regarded as a rank underdog in the presidential race, polled a surprising 42 percent of the vote and almost defeated Johnson. Soon afterward Senator Robert Kennedy of New York, the late President John Kennedy's brother, announced his candidacy and was regarded as a formidable opponent. Another presidential primary was scheduled to be held in Wisconsin, and Johnson's aides told him he would probably be defeated there. On top of this political bad news, Johnson's new Defense Secretary Clark Clifford told the president he now opposed any further bombing in Vietnam. And following hard on the heels of the disastrous American "victory" during the Tet offensive, General Westmoreland said he would need 200,000 additional troops.

Suddenly it all became too much for President Lyndon Johnson. On the evening of March 31, 1968, the president appeared on national television and announced that he was stopping the bombing of North Vietnam permanently except for a narrow corridor near the DMZ. He then announced his withdrawal from the presidential race.

At about the same time, President Johnson said that he had decided even before the Tet offensive to replace General Westmoreland as the field commander in Vietnam. This face-saving gesture enabled the president to bring Westmoreland home and promote him to the position of U.S. Army Chief of Staff. When General Abrams took over his new command he immediately began plans for a new Allied campaign to be called "Operation Complete Victory." Before the year was out Abrams had at his command almost 550,000 U.S. troops, 25,000 over Johnson's previously announced ceiling. U.S. combat deaths soon reached almost 25,000, and on Sunday, June 23, 1968, the war became the longest in United States history, surpassing the length of the American Revolution.

Somewhat surprisingly, President Johnson's bombing halt and his decision not to run for reelection brought Hanoi to the peace table in Paris on May 10. At the first meeting, however, the main discussions centered around what shape the peace table should be. A long table presented a problem regarding who sat at its head and foot. A circular table was finally decided upon. But as soon as both sides fully realized that neither side wanted to surrender, the peace parley broke up.

The Vietcong then staged a "mini-Tet" offensive, and General Abrams's offensive Operation Complete Victory turned into a defensive holding operation. Casualties ran high on both sides as the Vietcong again struck at more than one hundred cities, towns, and Allied military bases, and the United States resumed its aerial bombing offensive. The bombing of North Vietnam continued until November, when President Johnson again announced that it would end "permanently."

Johnson's second announcement of a bombing halt was regarded by many as an attempt to encourage Americans to vote for Vice-President Hubert Humphrey, who had been nominated by the Democrats as their presidential candidate in place of Johnson. Johnson, however, had virtually assured Humphrey's defeat when earlier in the campaign he had not allowed Humphrey to repudiate the Johnson administration's handling of the Vietnam War. At the same time, Republican presidential candidate Richard Nixon campaigned on a promise to bring home the American troops and end the war. On November 5, 1968, Nixon was elected president, winning over Humphrey by a narrow margin.

Nixon's program to end the war was called "Vietnamization." It took him almost a year after he took office to put Vietnamization into effect. When he did so he turned the Vietnam War into total disaster and defeat for the United States and South Vietnam.

8.
THE MY LAI MASSACRE

Shortly after Richard Nixon was inaugurated as president and before he could put his war-ending Vietnamization program into effect, a story broke in the American media that shocked the public. Apparently some U.S. soldiers in Vietnam had killed a whole village full of innocent women, children, and old men. Asked about the story at a press conference, President Nixon said: "It was a massacre all right. And under no circumstances was it justified."

The atrocity had actually occurred a full year earlier, on Saturday, March 16, 1968, at the Vietnamese village of My Lai. There several hundred noncombatant villagers—the official figure was later set at 347—had been systematically slaughtered by some members of an Americal Division infantry platoon led by a Lieutenant William L. Calley, Jr. President Nixon first heard about the affair in a letter from Vietnam veteran Ronald L. Ridenhour dated March 29, 1969, urging the president to look into persistent rumors about "something rather dark and bloody that did indeed occur sometime in March 1968 in a village called 'Pinkville' in the Republic of Vietnam."

Ridenhour had not been at My Lai. He was, however, a former member of Charlie Company to which Lieutenant Calley's platoon belonged, and a month after the atrocity occurred his former buddies told him about it. When he returned to the United States and was honorably discharged, Ridenhour wrote the story down as he had heard it and sent copies to President Nixon, the Secretary of Defense, Secretary of State, and key congressmen. It was at this point that the story broke in the media and an investigation was begun.

Charlie Company was a part of Task Force Barker headed by Lieutenant Colonel Frank A. Barker, Jr. The grunts of Charlie Company called My Lai "Pinkville" because the area it occupied was colored pink on the topographic military maps. Charlie Company had been in Vietnam for several months before the My Lai incident occurred. During that time about half of the company's 190 men had been hit by sniper fire or were seriously wounded or killed by Vietcong booby traps. They had experienced grim months of combat, more or less typical of those suffered by all infantry grunts in Vietnam. When Lieutenant Calley told his platoon they had orders from Company Commander Ernest Medina to clear out the Vietcong occupying Pinkville, it was like being alerted for any other mission.

Following a short artillery barrage on the village, Calley and his men were flown by helicopter to the landing zone outside My Lai, shortly after dawn on March 16. They were accompanied by two helicopter gunships called "Sharks." The Sharks fired thousands of rounds of ammunition into My Lai just before Calley's platoon, their M-16 rifles at the ready, sprang from the troop-carrying helicopters and raced toward the village. But there was no enemy return fire. There was, apparently, no enemy. Nevertheless, Calley ordered his men to round up all of the civilians at the center of the village. As soon as a sizable group of women, children, and old men were gathered there, Calley opened fire on them and ordered his men to do likewise. Most obeyed. Civilians who were slow in leaving their thatched huts, or "hootches" as the grunts called them, were blown to bits by grenades tossed through the doorways.

Then Calley's platoon moved through the village systematically shooting anything that moved. Dozens of victims were thrown into a drainage ditch and riddled by automatic rifle fire. Among these victims was a Buddhist priest holding a baby. According to testimony given at Lieutenant Calley's trial held later at Fort Benning, Georgia, the lieutenant hit the priest in the mouth with his rifle butt, shot him in the head, and then threw the baby into the ditch after the priest and shot it.

No Vietcong were ever seen by Calley's platoon in My Lai, yet the murder of innocent civilians went on for several hours.

Not all of the grunts took part in the massacre. One who did not was Sergeant Michael Bernhardt. "It was point-blank murder," he said later. "I said the hell with this. I'm not doing it. I didn't think it was a lawful order."

Another American who saw and objected to the civilian slaughter was Warrant Officer Hugh C. Thompson, Jr. Thompson was the pilot of an observation helicopter flying over My Lai. He announced over his radio that "if he saw the ground troops kill one more woman or child, he would start shooting the ground troops himself."

A short time later Thompson landed his helicopter

and asked the gunship pilots to join him. Two of them did so. They were Warrant Officers Jerry R. Culverhouse and Daniel R. Millians. The three pilots then managed to rescue a number of civilians and fly them to safety despite Calley's threats that "the only way you'll get them out is with a hand grenade." Thompson himself rescued sixteen children and was later awarded the Distinguished Flying Cross.

Despite the fact that there were numerous radio messages back and forth among the combat pilots and crewmen flying over My Lai that morning, as well as to rear echelon headquarters, no attempt was made by any senior officers to investigate and stop the massacre. Responsible for monitoring such messages were Major General Samuel Koster, Colonel Oran K. Henderson, and other high-ranking officers who flew over My Lai several times during the morning. But General Koster later testified that he "could not recall any details of the My Lai operation." Colonel Henderson testified that he had seen bodies of "several" civilians during one flight over My Lai and that he had immediately checked with Lieutenant Colonel Barker, the Task Force Commander. Henderson said that Barker had told him the civilians were killed by the artillery fire that preceded the ground attack. Unfortunately, Colonel Barker was killed in a helicopter crash several months after the My Lai massacre and long before an investigation got under way, so he could not testify about the "something rather dark and bloody" that occurred at My Lai.

The coverup of the My Lai massacre began almost immediately. First of all the body count had to be fabricated to indicate that the hundreds of dead civilians were members of the Vietcong. When it became apparent that this manufactured story could not possibly hold up, the number of dead civilians was attributed to the pre-dawn artillery barrage. Since this barrage had lasted only a few minutes, however, it was never made clear how it could have caused so many deaths. Nevertheless, Colonel Barker's superior officers in the American Division accepted his report, filed two weeks after the My Lai massacre, that the attack was "well planned, well executed, and successful."

And so the matter lay buried until Ronald Ridenhour wrote the letter that prompted the army investigation. As a result of the investigation twelve officers and enlisted men were charged with murder or assault with intent to commit murder at My Lai. After numerous long delays only Lieutenant Calley was found guilty. All of the rest of the accused were acquitted, or charges against them were dismissed. Calley was sentenced to life imprisonment, which was later reduced to twenty years, subject to review on March 29, 1971. General Koster, who had since become Superintendent of the Military Academy at West Point, was reduced in rank, censured, and ordered to return his Distinguished Service Medal.

The public reaction to Calley's conviction was a curious one. Many Americans apparently believed either that Calley was innocent or, if not, he had "given the 'gooks' or 'slopes' what they had coming to them." Furthermore, it seemed obvious to the man and woman in the street that Calley had been made the "fall guy" for high-ranking military officers who should have been found guilty also but had gone scot free. Shrewdly aware of public opinion, President Nixon declared that he would "personally review the case and finally decide it." Nixon never did so, but his statement appeased some critics of the Nixon administration for its role in the Calley conviction.

Commenting on the My Lai tragedy and its aftermath, Lieutenant General William R. Peers, who led the army's official inquiry into My Lai, perhaps summed up the affair best when he said, "To think that out of all those men, only one, Lieutenant William Calley, was brought to justice. And now he's practically a hero. It's a tragedy."

While there have been atrocities committed by both sides in almost all wars, this by no means excuses them. But then perhaps nothing excuses war itself, which may well be the greatest of atrocities against mankind. Even in Vietnam the My Lai massacre was not, unfortunately, an isolated incident. On the very same day that the My Lai incident occurred, a similar slaughter of fifty or so civilians is believed to have taken place in a nearby village. And in the battle of Hue during the Tet offensive the Vietcong were reported to have tortured and killed several hundred South Vietnamese civilians.

Nevertheless, such actions were by no means common among the soldiers on either side in the Vietnam War. When they occurred, they were what biologists call a "sport," which may be defined as "a sudden spontaneous change of a plant or animal from its normal type." The My Lai massacre, unforgivable as it was, was indeed a sudden, abnormal change from the way soldiers on both sides usually treated civilian noncombatants.

Much more common was the genuine concern shown for helpless civilians, especially children, as displayed by Warrant Officer Thompson in his rescue of the sixteen children at My Lai at the risk of his own life. All through the war countless American soldiers displayed similar consideration and love for Vietnamese children. One of these soldiers was Master Sergeant Bobbie Loeschner of the First Infantry Division's Second Brigade.

Sergeant Loeschner, a career soldier, had arrived in Vietnam late in 1965 and was stationed at a base camp at Long Binh. While on an infantry sweep through the countryside, Loeschner and his men were pinned down by mortar fire from a village. Returning the fire, they finally attacked the village and drove off the Vietcong. When they took over the village, the only living thing they found was a four-month-old Vietnamese baby boy buried under some rubble.

Sergeant Loeschner took the infant, who was slightly injured, back to his base camp. There the baby was nursed back to health and later placed in a Saigon orphanage. Loeschner visited the baby as regularly as his combat duties permitted, bringing him candy, food, and clothing.

Since Loeschner and his wife, Rosemarie, back in the United States had no children, he eventually decided— with her agreement—to adopt the boy. The adoption went through in the spring of 1966, and Nguyan Thien Quang became Bobbie Gene Loeschner, Jr.

When Sergeant Loeschner returned to the United States permanently—he had served two tours of duty in Vietnam—he and his wife and their Vietnamese son lived at several army camps. Young Bobbie officially became an American citizen when he was four.

Sergeant Loeschner retired from the army at Fort Leonard Wood, Missouri, in 1972. Later the Loeschners moved to Girard, Illinois, where Bobbie, Jr., grew up and attended the local schools and showed special interest in music and athletics. He began to play the guitar when he was just three, and by the time he was nine he had composed half a dozen songs. His athletic interests centered around baseball, which he played with great skill as he moved into high school in the late 1970s. As his adoptive father commented frequently, "Young Bobbie is at least *one* good thing that came out of the Vietnam War."

Unfortunately, the retired Sergeant Loeschner died of cancer in 1980. He was forty-five.

9.
VIETNAMIZATION—
AND DEFEAT

Ten months after he took office as president, Nixon finally announced his plan for the Vietnamization of the war. The plan was simple enough. What it meant was that all fighting against the Vietcong would be done by ARVN forces, and the United States would supply South Vietnam with the necessary money, food, and military supplies to carry on the war. Thus the role of the United States was to be essentially the same as it had been when the war began.

The problem was that there really could be no turning back of history's clock. The United States had paid dearly in blood and money for the conflict to date, to gain what at best could be called a stalemate. By March of 1969 the number of Americans killed in Vietnam passed the number of those killed in Korea—33,639. And the war was costing the United States more than $25 billion a year. This had caused an inflationary spiral that was threatening the country's economy.

While plans were still being made to wind down the use of American troops in the war, the North Vietnamese stepped up the flow of infiltrators into South Vietnam.

Consequently, there was still much bloody fighting for American grunts before they became disengaged from the Vietcong. One such engagement took place at what became known as "Hamburger Hill." It occurred in mid-May while stories of the My Lai massacre were very much in the news and causing public outcry.

Hamburger Hill was actually a small mountain near the border of Laos. Here the entrenched Vietcong withstood a week-long series of frontal infantry assaults by American and ARVN forces who suffered more than 350 casualties before Hamburger Hill was finally taken. Finally the Vietcong fled into their Laotian sanctuary, and a few days later the U.S. Army command announced that Hamburger Hill was being abandoned.

The nationwide reaction in the United States against such senseless sacrifice caused President Nixon to announce that in July 25,000 troops would be returned to the United States. Even the army admitted the attack was a blunder and Hamburger Hill worthless. Nixon further promised that by the end of 1969 another 85,000 troops would be withdrawn, and he planned on having "all of America's fighting forces out of Vietnam by 1970 or 1971 at the latest."

Meanwhile, formal peace talks were once again begun in Paris. On September 3, 1969, Ho Chi Minh died in Hanoi, and this fact combined with America's gradual troop withdrawal may have influenced the North Vietnamese leaders in their peace-seeking efforts. But if United States negotiators had expected a softening in North Vietnam's demands, they were badly mistaken. North Vietnam's premier, Pham Van Dong, had long been a close associate of Ho Chi Minh, and their aims were identical: the complete independence and unification of the whole of Vietnam, as well as freedom from foreign occupation or interference. Army Commander Giap, the National Liberation Front's representative in Hanoi, Nguyen Van Tien, and North Vietnam's chief negotiator at the Paris peace talks, Le Duc Tho, were also political hardliners. Consequently, the peace talks gave the American representatives, led by chief negotiators Henry Cabot Lodge and David K. E. Bruce, little cause for immediate optimism.

Adding to the United States' problems was South Vietnamese President Thieu's open skepticism regarding the ability of his ARVN forces to contain any major Vietcong offensive. He was reassured by the Nixon administration that United States air power would still be available to blunt any such Vietcong attack.

Nixon's reassurance about the continued use of American air power was not an idle one. It soon became perfectly clear that while Nixon would indeed pull American troops out of Vietnam, this did not mean that he intended to be the first U.S. president to lose a major war. What he was seeking, Nixon said, was "Peace with honor." If this meant "bombing North Vietnam back to the Stone Age," in the words of Air Force General Curtis LeMay, then so be it. Although National Foreign Policy Adviser Henry Kissinger wanted "to get out of the war as quietly as Johnson got us into it," he fully supported Nixon's back-to-the-Stone-Age bombing policy.

Beginning in 1969, the U.S. Air Force doubled the number of tons of bombs it had previously dropped on North and South Vietnam. It also played a key role in expanding the war into neighboring Cambodia and Laos. The bombing effort along with what General Westmoreland's successor, General Abrams, called an "Accelerated Pacification Campaign," brought about some of the most successful Allied military results of the war.

Following the Hamburger Hill incident, General Abrams withdrew both American and ARVN troops from any more so-called "border battles." Instead, he concentrated Allied efforts on clearing out small concentrations of Vietcong troops in the Mekong Delta area, as well as cutting enemy supply lines and destroying supply bases throughout South Vietnam. Although this all-out campaign caused wide destruction of villages and crops and created thousands of additional refugees, it was apparently successful in bringing large areas of South Vietnam under Allied control.

Once again, however, success was deceptive. After the Tet offensive the Vietcong returned to guerrilla warfare. With rare exceptions—such as at Hamburger Hill—the VC simply continued to infiltrate South Vietnam and avoided engaging in any major pitched battles. There was no question that the Vietcong had suffered severe casualties in the Tet attacks, and those casualties, along with the stepped-up American bombing campaign, caused the VC to lie low and bide their time against future offensives. The enemy was also well aware that the United States was gradually pulling its ground troops out of Vietnam, and maintaining a low level of activity until this trickle of departing troops became a flood made good sense to General Giap. Nevertheless, lack of powerful Vietcong resistance caused great optimism among American commanders as 1969 drew to a close. Back in the United States, President Nixon was quick to declare that the first steps in his Vietnamization program were "a great success."

In the spring of 1970 the ruler of Cambodia, Prince

Norodom Sihanouk, made an effort to get North Vietnam to stop using his country as a sanctuary for Vietcong troops. He did this by journeying to Russia to ask the Soviet leaders to put pressure on Hanoi to withdraw the Vietcong from Cambodia. While Sihanouk was in Moscow, one of his aides at home, General Lon Nol, seized control of the Cambodian government.

For years the U.S. Joint Chiefs of Staff had wanted to invade Cambodia and drive out the Vietcong, but both Presidents Johnson and Nixon had known that Prince Sihanouk would violently protest their bringing his country into the war. Now, however, Nixon knew that right-wing General Nol was a South Vietnamese sympathizer who would not object to an Allied move into Cambodia to drive the Vietcong from their sanctuaries there. Once again with Kissinger's approval—if not insistence —Nixon ordered just such an invasion. As soon as it was under way, Nixon told a nationwide radio and television audience, "For five years neither the United States nor South Vietnam has moved against the sanctuaries because we did not want to violate the territory of a neutral nation." No mention was made by the president of the more than 3,500 secret American air raids that had already been made on Cambodia in the past year.

The invasion of Cambodia had two immediate effects. First, as a "protective measure," half of Cambodia was taken over by the Vietcong. Second, the invasion caused the most violent antiwar demonstrations to that point in the United States. The U.S. Senate passed a resolution calling for the withdrawal of American troops from Cambodia and an end to aerial bombing there. On college and university campuses there was a virtual nationwide strike, and thousands of protesting students descended upon Washington where they picketed the White House.

Tragedy struck on the homefront when a bomb planted by a war protestor wrecked a building on the University of Wisconsin campus, killing one person and injuring several others. Also two students were killed and several were wounded at Mississippi's Jackson State University when police opened fire on war protestors there. But the most memorable campus tragedy resulting from Nixon's announcement of the invasion of Cambodia occurred at Kent State University in Ohio. There, National Guardsmen fired on student demonstrators gathered on the campus Commons, killing four students and wounding nine others. It was not until March of 1974 that eight guardsmen were indicted for their part in this unexplained attack, and then a federal judge dismissed all charges against them for violating the students' civil rights. Later, the state of Ohio agreed to pay victims or their parents $675,000, and guardsmen offered their official regret for their part in the incident.

The antiwar spirit at home gradually began to spill over into Vietnam, where discipline among American troops was frequently difficult to maintain. While no widespread mutiny was ever threatened, here and there marked reluctance to obey combat orders was displayed. Occasionally units flatly refused to try to make their way through newly discovered Vietcong tunnels that might still be occupied by the enemy, and now and then enlisted men "voted" on whether or not to follow combat orders.

Throughout much of the war, enlisted men displayed more than the normal resentment of their officers. Much of this was caused by the fact that officers were sent to Vietnam for six month tours of duty, which was just half the length of time served by enlisted men. Not only did the grunts resent these shorter tours, but the spirit and morale of combat units suffered from the frequent changes in leadership.

Many officers were also "career conscious." This meant they were volunteers or military academy graduates who planned on making a career of military service. To advance rapidly in rank they needed a period of combat experience in wartime on their service records. Consequently, many of them were interested only in getting into and out of combat as fast and as safely as possible. This was by no means true of all officers, but unfortunately it was true of many.

Most enlisted men, on the other hand, were draftees who wanted only to survive the jungle hell they found themselves in and return to "the world"—as the grunts called civilian life back in the United States. Furthermore, there was a serious imbalance of black soldiers among the enlisted men. Most of the young men of draft age who could afford to go to college—and thus be deferred from military service—were white. As a result, blacks saw the Vietnam conflict not merely as a rich man's war and a poor man's fight, but as a white man's war and a black man's fight.

In the 1970s the enlisted men's reaction against the war and resentment of their officers began to boil over into frequent "fragging" incidents. Fragging got its name from live fragmentation grenades which mutinous grunts took to tossing into officers' living quarters, causing severe casualties. Although this vicious practice was isolated, it was a constant threat that did little to improve officer-enlisted man relationships.

The low level of troop morale was also displayed by

the wide use of drugs. Marijuana was grown throughout Vietnam and was consequently easy and cheap to obtain. Many if not most soldiers smoked it. A study made by the U.S. military command in 1971 estimated that 10 percent of the American troops were using heroin and half of them were confirmed addicts. The Vietnamese heroin, unfortunately, was extremely pure, which increased the incidence of addiction. Some use of other hard drugs such as opium was also reported by the military command Drug Abuse Task Force, which was organized to combat the growing menace to American servicemen.

American troops, as the Senate had demanded, were withdrawn from Cambodia in July of 1970. In a further move to prevent the Nixon administration from undertaking any new adventures in Indochina, Congress, late in the year, denied military funds for the use of American troops in Laos. And in an attempt to reestablish its constitutional war-making rights, Congress ended the year by repealing the Gulf of Tonkin Resolution. This move was described by media commentators as a piece of closing-the-barn-door-after-the-horse-is-stolen legislation.

The Nixon–Kissinger Vietnamization program had its first real test in February of 1971, when 16,000 ARVN troops aided by American air support invaded Laos. This so-called "incursion" was originally named the "Dewey Canyon Operation." But General Abrams feared this name might imply to antiwar demonstrators that the operation was part of a continued American effort. He then renamed it the "Lam Son Operation" after Lam Son, a heroic ARVN colonel.

The stated purpose of the Lam Son Operation was to disrupt the Vietcong troop and supply movements along the Ho Chi Minh Trail that led through part of Laos. For years the U.S. Joint Chiefs had favored such a move, just as they had long favored and were delighted with the "incursion" into Laos.

During the first two weeks the ARVN troops met with little opposition as they moved into Laos. Then, suddenly, several divisions of North Vietnamese troops struck with everything in their arsenal—tanks, rockets, and artillery. Desperately, the ARVN commanders called for American defensive air strikes. They were not always successful in making clear to the fighter-bomber pilots where the attacks should be made, but the U.S. gave the ARVN forces massive close-in bombing support and succeeded in killing perhaps 10,000 Vietcong. ARVN losses were high, with some units suffering 50 percent casualties. U.S. helicopters flew in replacements, but soon ARVN commanders were asking permission to withdraw. Despite a South Vietnamese casualty rate that was "worse than Tet," according to General Abrams's deputy commander, General Frederick Weyland, no withdrawal was allowed. The United States had said the ARVN would succeed in Laos and a retreat was "unacceptable." Many ARVN infantrymen simply broke and ran, their retreat covered by U.S. planes.

At mid-March when the Lam Son disaster drew to a merciful close, numerous ARVN battalions were unable to fight any longer. Overall ARVN casualties were about 10,000 men. This did not include desertions, which ran as high as 12,000 men a month. Following Lam Son, traffic on the Ho Chi Minh Trail was greater than ever.

Undaunted, President Nixon announced to the nation in April that "Vietnamization has succeeded."

In mid-June the Pentagon Papers were released to the American public, causing the clamor for peace to reach a new peak. In August President Nixon sent William J. Porter to Paris to replace David Bruce as chief negotiator, but the peace talks remained stalled. The Nixon-Kissinger response to the continuing stalemate was to continue to seek an honorable peace by escalating the bombing campaign.

Nixon did, however, continue to withdraw American ground troops. By early 1972 the number was down to 70,000, at which time the Vietcong launched a major offensive against South Vietnam. Kissinger confidently called this offensive, "Hanoi's last throw of the dice." This it very nearly was—but for Saigon, not Hanoi.

This spring offensive was every bit as big as the Tet offensive, but it resembled Tet in size only. There were no coffins filled with ammunition, and the Vietcong did not strike at numerous places simultaneously. Instead, they swarmed across the DMZ demarcation line, and in massive frontal assaults captured dozens of key South Vietnamese strongholds and moved to within sixty miles of Saigon. The four-pronged advance moved forward on a broad front overrunning such important provincial capitals as Quang Tri, Am Loc, and Dak To. One column of the advance, led by Soviet-manufactured tanks, roared out of Cambodia, threatening to cut the peninsula in half.

The only way the North Vietnamese were stopped was through the use of an unprecedented amount of U.S. air power. The advancing Vietcong columns were attacked relentlessly by air, and both Hanoi and Haiphong were subjected to saturation bombing. Like President Johnson, President Nixon had shied away from interfering with the international shipping in Haiphong harbor and the railway lines leading out of China, through fear of bringing China and Russia openly into the war. Now, however, Nixon threw such cautions aside. He ordered Haiphong harbor mined and blockaded, and the railway lines bombed close to the Chinese border.

Fortunately, if not miraculously, neither Russia nor China did anything but register formal objections to the U.S. actions. And gradually the Vietcong's massive drive against South Vietnam began to falter. But the Vietcong ground attacks and the American aerial onslaught continued all summer, resulting in the loss of hundreds of thousands of military and civilian lives on both sides.

Finally, in October, Le Duc Tho notified Henry Kissinger that he was willing to resume serious peace talks in Paris. The North Vietnamese decision was based partially on the failure of their military effort to overrun South Vietnam, and partially on the fact that once the United States was out of Vietnam there would be very little the Nixon administration could do to stop North Vietnam from taking over the whole country. President Nixon was more than eager for immediate peace, because he was running for reelection against Senator George McGovern of South Dakota, a favorite among the antiwar electorate. McGovern's campaign slogan was, "Don't let this man [Nixon] fool you again," and it had been winning McGovern a large following.

On election eve, however, McGovern had the rug pulled out from under his presidential hopes when Kissinger announced to the world: "Peace is at hand."

The peace talks had been delayed because Le Duc Tho had insisted that Vietnam's President Thieu be replaced with a coalition government before an agreement could be reached. When this demand was withdrawn by North Vietnam, Kissinger made his historic announcement, in mid-October.

In early November Nixon won a landslide victory over McGovern.

Immediately after the election the world began to wonder why a cease-fire in Vietnam had not occurred. Soon it became clear that peace was definitely not at hand. South Vietnam's President Thieu had refused to go along with the peace agreement because it was, he said, "surrender of the South Vietnamese people to the Communists." He insisted upon an ironclad promise by both North Vietnam and the United States that force would not be used to unite Vietnam. Such a promise would prevent him from being ousted by a North Vietnamese takeover. If this promise was not made, Thieu threatened that South Vietnam would carry on the war by itself. On its part, North Vietnam began to back down on its earlier agreement to turn over to the United States the hundreds of American prisoners of war as soon as a cease-fire was signed. Some POWs had been in North Vietnam prison camps for many years, and their freedom was a major issue among Americans.

Angry at both Thieu and Le Duc Tho, Nixon warned North Vietnam's Premier Pham Van Dong that unless a cease-fire was signed within seventy-two hours the blockade of Haiphong harbor and the saturation bombing of Hanoi would be resumed.

Pham Van Dong refused to reply to this ultimatum, and the result was what historian William Manchester described as "the most savage chapter in the long history of American involvement in Vietnam. Hanoi was pounded around the clock by every type of American aircraft in every kind of weather. Using 100 of the huge green and brown B-52s, U.S. airmen flew over 1,400 sorties in the first week alone. Americans were stunned."

Not only the Americans were stunned, of course; so were the North Vietnamese and, for that matter, the entire world. This savage aerial blitz became notorious as "Nixon's Christmas bombing of Hanoi." Actually there was a thirty-six-hour halt in the bombing at Christmas, but it was resumed in all its fury as soon as the holiday ended.

Although American and world opinion was strongly opposed to it, the Christmas bombing did force North Vietnam back to the peace table. A contributing factor in Hanoi's request to resume the peace talks was probably the fact that China and Russia would not give any indication that they would intervene in North Vietnam's behalf. In fact Chinese and Soviet leaders were urging Premier Pham Van Dong to end the war.

When Hanoi urgently requested new peace talks, Nixon declared a bombing halt and agreed to sign a cease-fire agreement. Nixon and Kissinger maintained later that the Christmas bombing had been halted because Hanoi had finally realized that the United States could impose its will on North Vietnam. This is doubtful. It is more likely that the bombing was halted because Nixon and Kissinger knew that the new Democratic Congress would allow no more funds to be used for bombing in Vietnam.

On January 23, 1973, Henry Kissinger and Le Duc Tho initialed a formal cease-fire agreement for Vietnam. The agreement ending hostilities was officially signed on January 27. The last American troops left South Vietnam at the end of March. And in April, what were said to be the last American prisoners of war came home to the United States.

The war in Vietnam was officially over.

Its aftermath, however, was not.

10.
AFTERMATH

The United States and Indochina were to suffer from the Vietnam War, both physically and emotionally, for years to come.

In blood and money the longest war in the long history of America's wars cost the nation some 46,000 men killed in battle, more than 300,000 wounded, and more than $141 billion. An additional 10,000 men died in Vietnam from noncombat causes such as accidents and illness. Among the wounded some 74,000 were crippled with more than 50 percent disability. Another 1,200 men were reported missing in action. Between 1963 and 1973 a total of 2,600,000 Americans served in Vietnam.

If President Nixon had ended the war when he came into office in January 1969 by making the same concessions to North Vietnam that he ended up making in January 1973, he would have saved much of this blood and treasure. More than 15,000 American men were killed and more than $57 billion were spent on the war after Nixon took office. The Nixon-Kissinger "Peace with Honor" goal, which was never achieved, was indeed an expensive one.

It was, however, President Johnson who was mainly responsible for making the conflict an American war. Cooing like a Dove in the 1964 election campaign, he won a landslide victory only to turn into a Hawk. He then committed more and more American troops to the conflict and insisted that they would come home only "when they nail the coonskin to the wall."

The American military leaders, of course, bore a major responsibility for the continued troop escalation which, they always assured the president, would bring victory. Even when American troops in Vietnam passed the half-million mark, requests were made for an additional 200,-000 men—requests which Johnson, finally, turned down.

The United States also suffered thousands of civilian casualties. These included not only the unfortunate few who died in antiwar demonstrations but also the 21,000 youths who were indicted for draft evasion. Of these some 7,500 went to prison. In a kind of twilight zone between civilian and military casualties could be included the 425,000 men who deserted from all of the military services from 1966 onward. About 390,000 of these were eventually returned to "military control," where they received sentences ranging from company punishment to five years in prison. By the end of the war more than 32,000 deserters were still at large.

Some 200,000 South Vietnamese soldiers were killed in the conflict, and about half a million were wounded. The civilian toll was even greater. Official estimates ran as high as half a million South Vietnamese civilians killed and an additional million wounded. It should be emphasized that these are only estimates gathered through interviews with some of the tens of thousands of refugees from destroyed cities, towns, and villages.

America's South Korea, Thai, and Australian combat allies did not get off lightly in the conflict. They suffered more than 5,000 killed and some 12,000 wounded.

North Vietnamese casualty figures were more difficult to obtain by Western observers. At least a million North Vietnamese soldiers were killed in combat and possibly 3 million were wounded. The number of North Vietnamese civilian deaths is unknown, but more than 50,-000 were killed during one period of intensive bombing alone—the eighteen months of President Johnson's bombing escalation in 1967 and 1968. It should be noted that this excludes the Nixon-Kissinger back-to-the-Stone-Age bombing campaign of the early 1970s.

An unestimated number of people in Cambodia and Laos, where no records were kept, also suffered severely from the war—and were still suffering from the war's aftermath into the 1980s. The invasion and continued aerial bombing of Cambodia and Laos—especially Cambodia—were two of the most controversial American acts of the war. Their effects were also the most lingering.

When the cease-fire agreement was signed in Paris in 1973, it left a loophole regarding the bombardment of Cambodia and Laos. The United States continued to aid South Vietnam in this bombardment. Its continuation led to further violations of the agreement on both sides, and soon the fighting was as bloody as ever in what amounted to a virtual civil war in Indochina. The Nixon administration provided South Vietnam with more than $500 million in guns, ammunition, and aircraft. The United States also continued to be the only support for the economy of South Vietnam.

Finally, however, in April of 1975 the ARVN collapsed

and South Vietnam's President Thieu was faced with being ousted. In Cambodia, Lon Nol's regime was also threatened with collapse. At this juncture former Vice President Gerald R. Ford, who had replaced Nixon as president following Nixon's resignation, tried to get Congress to allot more funds to support Thieu and Lon Nol. But Congress refused. It and the American people had had quite enough of war in Indochina.

Although there was no formal agreement among the countries involved, this decision by Congress to cut off all war funds was actually the end of United States involvement in the Vietnam War. North Vietnam soon overran the whole of South Vietnam, including the capital city of Saigon and the American embassy there. The end was a sorrowful sight for patriotic Americans. The TV-viewing public witnessed the last American officials and marines being lifted by helicopter from the embassy roof as the Vietcong stormed into the city. So desperate were many former South Vietnamese allies to be evacuated that they tried to hang onto the landing gear skids of the rescue helicopters. Other South Vietnamese could be seen being clubbed off the walls of the embassy compound when they tried to scale them and enter the rescue area. In all, there were more than 1,000 American civilian evacuees and 900 marines airlifted by the fleet of helicopters to ships standing offshore. Many South Vietnamese officials also managed to escape by air from other parts of the country, but most were left behind. Some of these later escaped by sea. The last marines left the embassy roof on April 30, 1975. Soon afterward Saigon was renamed Ho Chi Minh City.

Nixon's resignation as president followed his involvement in what was called the "Watergate Affair," a part of which grew directly out of the Vietnam War. Daniel Ellsberg's release of the Pentagon Papers to the press in mid-June of 1971 caused Nixon's aides to want to find out all they could about him. If Ellsberg could release Top Secret information to the press that was damaging to the Johnson administration—and the courts would allow newspapers to publish it—someone else might be able to leak similar damaging information about the Nixon administration—something like information about the secret bombing of Cambodia. Consequently, Nixon's aides wanted to obtain damaging information about Ellsberg that might be used at his trial or leaked to the media to destroy his reputation. Out of this grew an effort by some Nixon aides (called the "Plumbers' Unit") to burglarize the office of Ellsberg's psychiatrist in Los Angeles. The burglary was committed in the fall of 1971, but the Plumbers found nothing they could use.

Later, during the election campaign of 1972, a second Plumbers' Unit broke into the Democratic Party's national headquarters in the Watergate apartment and office complex in Washington. This time they were attempting to plant "bugs" in the phones of Nixon's political opponents and also to steal documents that might disclose his opponents' campaign plans. The Plumbers were caught in the midst of their attempted burglary. They were not immediately linked to Nixon and his aides, however, and Nixon went on to win his overwhelming victory over George McGovern.

It was not until 1974, in fact, that it became known publicly that Nixon had learned of the Watergate break-in a few days after it happened and had immediately ordered a coverup of the burglary. During the course of these Watergate disclosures it also became known that

Nixon's aides had planned and carried out the earlier burglary of Ellsberg's psychiatrist's office. Faced with impeachment, Nixon resigned as president on August 8, 1974, and was succeeded the next day by Gerald Ford.

National Security Adviser and later Secretary of State Henry Kissinger was not involved in the Watergate affair. He was deeply involved, however, in the wartime aerial bombing and invasion of Cambodia, and was widely blamed for the subsequent tragedy that took place in that country.

Kissinger claimed at the time and later in his memoirs that the bombing and invasion of Cambodia were justified and necessary. In fact, he said, "There was no alternative." He further justified the American attacks on a neutral country by insisting that the area attacked "was no longer Cambodian in any practical sense" since it had been used as a sanctuary by the Vietcong for so long. He concluded by asserting that the attacks "achieved our main goals."

One of these goals was to make it easier for the United States to withdraw from Vietnam and thus save American lives, evidently regardless of what it did to Cambodian lives. But, Kissinger claimed, "Cambodia was *not* a moral issue. What we faced was an essential tactical choice." Apparently it was not a moral issue with the judges either who later awarded him the Nobel Peace Prize for the settlement he negotiated for the Vietnam War. Le Duc Tho, who was awarded a share of the coveted Nobel Prize, declined to accept it.

Kissinger's critics said that if there had been no invasion of Cambodia by the United States, it was highly unlikely that North Vietnam would later have tried to overrun that country. But this is by no means certain.

There were also other political forces at work there.

When the United States Congress refused to grant any more funds to prop up the South Vietnamese and Cambodian regimes of Thieu and Lon Nol in the spring of 1975, both governments fell and their leaders went into exile. The exiled Thieu was especially bitter over what he regarded as the United States' final "betrayal" of South Vietnam. After Kissinger's memoirs were published in 1979, Thieu lashed out at the former Secretary of State for having negotiated the "peace of the grave" in Vietnam.

Thieu also pointed out that the Paris peace agreement had resulted in starvation and torture for many South Vietnamese and confinement in "concentration camps" for thousands of others. Actually, what Thieu called concentration camps were called "reeducation camps" by the new Vietnamese government, and thousands of former South Vietnamese soldiers were indeed sent to them. In addition, hundreds of thousands of middle-class South Vietnamese lost their farms, homes, and businesses and were forced to flee the country. Some fled overland to Thailand or by small boats to Malaysia, Hong Kong, Indonesia, and even Australia, several thousand miles away. Many eventually reached the United States where they sought asylum. The pitiful plight of these "boat people" became a cause of international concern for several years after the war.

Of equal if not even greater international concern was the postwar fate of the Cambodian people. When Lon Nol's Cambodian regime fell, he was replaced by Pol Pot and Cambodia was renamed Kampuchea. Pol Pot headed the country's revolutionary forces which were called the Khmer Rouge. The Khmer are an ancient people in

Cambodia, dating back to the country's beginning. In taking over the government they seemed intent on turning the nation back into a primitive society. For four years under the Khmer Rouge there was a reign of mass terror and murder in an attempt to wipe out every "educated" person in the country. Any person who could read or write, anyone who spoke English or French, even anyone who wore eyeglasses was killed. A serious attempt was also made to break up all family units and to make the entire society live in communes. Anyone who owned a small cooking pot that could be used to make food for a single family could be sentenced to death.

Finally, in what they claimed was an effort to end the Khmer Rouge "government of madmen" and to stabilize the country, the Vietnamese invaded Cambodia in December of 1978. They installed a puppet regime responsible to Hanoi which was headed by President Heng Samrin. Unfortunately, the fate of the Cambodian people did not seem to improve to any marked degree under the new regime.

By late 1979 the Cambodian economy was destroyed and there was little or no food available. It was estimated that as many as five million of Cambodia's original eight million people had been slaughtered by the Khmer Rouge. Now, under the Vietnamese, the remaining Cambodians apparently faced starvation. The United States was in the forefront of the many Western nations offering food and medical aid to these starving millions, but for a time the politics involved in the situation made it unlikely that the international assistance would arrive in time. The Thai government was reluctant to allow the Cambodians into its country for fear of being drawn into the fighting between the Vietnamese and the Khmer

Rouge. The Vietnamese resisted allowing food and medicine into Cambodia because it might fall into the hands of the Khmer Rouge whom the Vietnamese were trying to destroy. As a result, the extinction of an entire people was threatened in Cambodia.

As the 1980s began, however, there was some indication that this tragic situation was changing. Thailand allowed more and more Cambodian refugees inside its borders. Food supplies were getting into Cambodia itself through such international agencies as World Vision, UNICEF, the Red Cross, OXFAM, and the World Council of Churches. According to representatives of these international relief agencies who were on the scene, some of this food was going to the Vietnamese occupation forces, but by no means all of it. Most, in fact, seemed to be going to the Cambodian people who were showing some signs of recovery. In addition, people were being allowed back into the capital city of Phnom Penh, which had become a ghost city under Pol Pot, with more than a million Cambodians driven from the city by the Khmer Rouge. By 1980 perhaps 150,000 had returned.

Some observers reported that Vietnam was providing aid to Kampuchea, and the Vietnamese had promised that they would eventually get out of the country. It remained to be seen whether the Vietnamese would indeed withdraw and whether the future existence of the Cambodians as a people would become a reality.

Nearly a decade after he returned from Vietnam, an American veteran of the conflict was asked what he regretted most about the Vietnam War. "They never gave us our parade," he said.

How true this wry comment was. When the Vietnam War ended, the traditional, somewhat grudging acceptance of the United States military by the American people turned into bitter and open disdain. Another Vietnam veteran who had lost an arm in combat was stopped on the street one day by a young civilian and asked, "Lose that in Vietnam?" The veteran nodded. "Serves you right," he was told.

The longest American war was also the least popular, and many American people seemed to want to take out the war's unpopularity on its veterans. In fact, this situation was so bad that many job-seeking veterans found they had a better chance of getting work if they never mentioned their war records. "Americans don't like losers," another veteran said. "Maybe that had something to do with it. Or maybe it was like the messenger bringing the bad news being killed just because he was the bearer of bad tidings. In any event, I know we 'Nam vets were bad news."

Not only were there no parades for returning Vietnam veterans, but in many instances their own government seemed to have forgotten them. In the mid-1970s the Veterans Administration fell months behind in the disbursement of educational benefit checks. Compensation for veterans who claimed to have become ill because of their exposure to the chemical defoliant Agent Orange was denied. Little or nothing was done for the many veterans who had returned home emotionally troubled and addicted to drugs and alcohol. As a result, some veterans frankly admitted they had been "suckers" to have fought in the war at all.

In 1979 President Jimmy Carter decided that it was about time that the Vietnam veterans had their parade.

He announced the first Vietnam Veterans' Week to be observed late in May.

"The nation still has a moral debt to these boys who served in Southeast Asia," President Carter said in announcing the week of tribute. "It's time," he added, "to recognize Vietnam-era veterans for their service."

As the new decade of the 1980s began, the veterans also took action on their own behalf. A national Vietnam Veterans of America organization was formed and successfully pressed for jobs, education, health care, and counseling. The federal government in turn revitalized the Veterans Administration under its new administrator, Max Cleland, who had lost both legs and an arm in Vietnam, and announced the opening of counseling centers throughout the country. Congress showed new awareness of the plight of veterans still bearing the psychological scars of combat with a $25 million package, including expanded drug and alcohol rehabilitation programs. Nineteen congressmen who had served in Vietnam formed a caucus to push legislation that would extend educational, job training, and other benefits from ten to twenty years for those who had served in Southeast Asia. The United States Air Force also began to conduct a lengthy study of the health of servicemen who had been subjected to Agent Orange.

American public opinion about the Vietnam War continued to be divided for years after the last grunt left Vietnam. The fact that it was the first war the United States had ever lost was difficult for many Americans to accept. They kept looking around for scapegoats, someone or something to blame other than the United States itself—for the defeat and for the cost in men and money. They found it almost impossible to believe that the

United States, with all of its military might, could actually have been defeated in what amounted to a guerrilla war. But it was.

Many Americans agreed with the so-called "hardliners" in the military establishment who claimed that the United States never should have lost the war. The United States military forces, according to the hardliners, were always forced to fight a "no win" war in Vietnam. These military forces, it was claimed, should have been allowed to invade Cambodia and Laos and to use any and all weapons at their disposal, including "small" tactical atomic bombs against North Vietnam. They pointed to North Vietnam's postwar take-over of much of Indochina as proof that the Domino Theory was correct and that the Communists were determined to gain control of the whole of Southeast Asia. This never would have happened, according to the hardliners, if the United States had been allowed to win the war in Vietnam.

Then there were those Americans—perhaps the majority—who claimed that the United States lost the war because it was "the wrong war, at the wrong place, at the wrong time." They firmly believed that the Vietnam War began as a nationalistic fight by the Vietnamese for independence, a fight that later grew into a civil war. In neither case, they insisted, did the United States have any legal or moral right to intervene: self-determination was the right and privilege of the Vietnamese, no matter what form of government they chose. It was American intervention, the people who held this point of view claimed, that had led to needless wartime killing and devastation and postwar bloodbaths such as that in Cambodia.

Was there any way to reconcile these two viewpoints? Perhaps not. But with the passage of time the people of the United States showed some signs of coming to terms with themselves about the Vietnam War. By the early 1980s the people who had once held such flatly opposite opinions about the justices and injustices of the tragic conflict in Vietnam gradually began to modify their positions somewhat. A final judgment would have to be made by future generations.

FURTHER READING

During the Vietnam War and for many years afterward there were very few books available for younger readers about that conflict. Consequently, most of the books listed here are for more mature readers.

The book that best catches the sometimes insane atmosphere of the war is Michael Herr's *Dispatches* (New York: Avon Books, 1978). In many ways this is the best war book I have ever read, ranking with Stephen Crane's *Red Badge of Courage* on the Civil War and James Jones's *From Here to Eternity* on World War II. (Strictly speaking Jones's book is pre-World War II, but it captures the army atmosphere in truly classic fashion.)

Perhaps equally good are Frances FitzGerald's *Fire in the Lake* (New York: Vintage Books, 1973) and David Halberstam's *The Best and the Brightest* (Greenwich, Conn.: Fawcett Publications, 1973). Neither book carries the war through to its conclusion, but each has special merits. The FitzGerald book is especially valuable for picturing the roles of the Americans and Vietnamese in the war. The Halberstam book deals with the United States' role in the war along with other aspects of the

Kennedy and Johnson presidential administrations. Halberstam was among the best of the reporters who covered the war in Vietnam, and one of the most violently opposed to it.

The best book for young people on the French in Indochina is Peter A. Poole's *Dien Bien Phu, 1954: The Battle That Ended the First Indochina War* (New York: Franklin Watts, 1972). This book does a remarkably good job with the Battle of Dien Bien Phu itself, as well as filling in the background of French colonialism in Indochina. Other excellent books on Dien Bien Phu—but definitely for more sophisticated readers—are Bernard B. Fall's *Hell in a Very Small Place* (New York: J. B. Lippincott, 1967) and Jules Roy's *The Battle of Dien Bien Phu* (New York: Harper & Row, 1965). Fall was one of the most sensitive writers covering the war. Unfortunately, he was killed by a land mine. His *Last Reflections on a War* (New York: Schocken Books, 1972) was published after his death and puts the conflict in historical perspective.

Younger readers will probably be interested in Robin Moore's *The Green Berets* (New York: Crown Publishers, 1965). This is fiction based on fact and was later made into a movie starring John Wayne that was much criticized by antiwar readers who protested its romanticizing of the war. The book does read pretty much like an adventure, and although there is much blood and gore, the blood and gore does not seem real. Casualties occur much as they do on TV, with a curious antiseptic quality rather than like a bad automobile accident which is what war casualties are really like. The book does, however, show how the Green Berets were trained and how they operated.

A much more realistic piece of fiction is Philip

Caputo's *A Rumor of War* (New York: Holt, Rinehart and Winston, 1977). Caputo was a combat veteran.

The best book on the My Lai massacre is Seymour M. Hersh's *Cover-Up: The Army's Secret Investigation of the Massacre at My Lai* (New York: Random House, 1972). Hersh won the Pulitzer Prize for breaking the My Lai story, and his book carefully documents that tragedy and its aftermath. Probably for specialists only is Joseph Goldstein's *The My Lai Massacre and Its Cover-Up: Beyond the Reach of Law?*, which is essentially a survey of the General William R. Peers's Commission Report on My Lai (New York: The Free Press, Macmillan, 1976).

The best book on the Daniel Ellsberg disclosures is Neil Sheehan and F. W. Kenworthy's *The Pentagon Papers As Published by The New York Times* (New York: Bantam Books, 1971).

William Manchester's *The Glory and the Dream* (New York: Bantam Books, 1975) is an absolutely marvelous narrative history of America from 1932 to 1972. The latter chapters contain much clear and concise information on the Vietnam War and the presidential administrations involved in it. This book should be used as a classroom textbook.

Among the best books about President Johnson and his role in the Vietnam War are *Lyndon Johnson and the American Dream* by Doris Kearns (New York: Signet, New American Library, 1976) and *Lyndon B. Johnson: The Exercise of Power*, by Rowland Evans and Robert Novak (New York: Signet, New American Library, 1968). President Nixon's involvement in the Vietnam War and Watergate is exhaustively covered in Theodore H. White's *Breach of Faith: The Fall of Richard Nixon* (New York: Atheneum Publishers, 1975).

The most elaborate book on the war is *The Vietnam War: The Illustrated History of the Conflict in Southeast Asia* (New York: Crown Publishers, 1979), edited by Ray Bonds. Young readers will certainly be interested in the photographs, drawings, maps, and charts which illustrate activities on both sides during the conflict. The articles themselves—the book's text is not so much a consecutive history as it is a collection of articles about the war—should be taken with several grains of salt since they are heavily pro-Pentagon.

Two excellent paperback histories of the United States that deal with the Vietnam War have been published by Penguin. They are Stephen E. Ambrose's *Rise to Globalism: American Foreign Policy 1938–1976,* Revised Edition (New York: Penguin Books, 1976) and Peter N. Carroll and David W. Noble's *The Free and the Unfree: A New History of the United States* (New York: Penguin Books, 1977). These are certainly for more advanced readers, but the Ambrose book especially presents a clear picture of the Vietnam War and America's role in it.

A good book about guerrilla warfare is *The Dirty Wars* (New York: Delacorte Press, 1968), edited by Donald Robinson. A realistic account of what it meant to be a prisoner of war in Vietnam is Major James N. Rowe's *Five Years to Freedom* (Boston: Little, Brown, 1976). A valuable study of Vietnam veterans in postwar America is John Helmer's *Bringing the War Home* (New York: The Free Press, Macmillan, 1974).

Something of what it was like in North Vietnam during the war is told by Harrison E. Salisbury in *Behind the Lines —Hanoi: December 23–January 7* (New York: Harper & Row, 1967). Salisbury was a *New York Times* correspondent who had the unique wartime experience of being allowed to visit the enemy capital and interview several of Ho Chi Minh's top aides.

Both sides of the Cambodian controversy are covered by Henry Kissinger in his memoirs, *White House Years* (New York: Little, Brown, 1979) and by William Shawcross in *Sideshow* (New York: Pocket Books, 1979).

A clear explanation of the Cold War and how it led to our becoming involved in Vietnam is contained in Louis J. Halle's *The Cold War As History* (New York: Harper & Row, 1967). Halle's was a sane voice in a mad world. It should have been listened to more carefully.

My own books, *The United States in World War II* and *The United States in the Korean War* (New York: Abelard-Schuman, 1963 and 1964), are suggested as background reading for young people on the Cold War and America's early role in Southeast Asia.

INDEX

Abrams, Creighton W., 96, 100, 101, 113–14, 118
aerial warfare
under Johnson, 33, 35, 39, 49–54, 62, 77, 94, 98–99, 100, 101, 127
under Nixon, 113–14, 119, 120–21, 122–23, 127, 129, 130
World War II comparisons of, 49, 50, 67–68
Agent Orange, 50–51, 134, 135
Aiken, George, 76, 95
Ambrose, Stephen, 74
American Civil Liberties Union, 72
American Revolutionary War, 56, 69
antiaircraft batteries, 52, 53
antiwar criticism, 67, 69–72, 74–76, 112, 115–18, 119, 121, 123, 126
Tet offensive and, 92–93
ARVN (Army of the Republic of Vietnam), 17, 19–20, 29, 30, 31, 38, 73, 74, 75, 77–78, 91, 95, 126, 127
in Lam Sol disaster, 118–19

Vietnamization and, 111, 112, 113
atomic bomb, 3, 21, 22, 23, 136
atrocities, 59, 67, 103–8

Baez, Joan, 71
Barker, Frank A., Jr., 104, 106, 107
Bay of Pigs invasion, 27
Bellow, Saul, 71
Berlin Blockade (1948), 23
Berlin Wall, 27
Bernhardt, Michael, 105
B-52 bombers, 39, 60, 123
blacks, as draftees, 117
"boat people," 131
body counts, 77–78, 79, 95
booby traps, 58–59
Bruce, David K. E., 113
Buddhists, 19, 29–30, 38

Calder, Alexander, 71
Calley, William L., Jr., 103–8
Cambodia, 3, 4, 114–15, 130–31, 136
bombings of, 113, 115, 127, 129, 130

postwar fate of, as
Kampuchea, 131–33
Vietcong and, 59–61, 115,
120
Vietnamese invasion of
(1978), 132–33
campuses, antiwar protests on,
70, 71, 115–16
Cam Ranh Bay, 91
Carter, Jimmy, 134–35
Castro, Fidel, 26–28
Central Highlands area, 59–61,
78–79
Chiang Kai-shek, 6, 24
China, People's Republic of, 3,
5–6, 24, 121, 123
North Vietnamese aided by,
6–7, 8, 51–52, 59
"Chopper War," 54
Churchill, Winston, 21
CIA (Central Intelligence
Agency)
in Cuban crisis, 26–27
in Vietnam, 28, 30, 78
Clark, Mark, 68
Cleland, Max, 135
Clifford, Clark M., 96, 100
Cold War, 21–30
Asia and, 24, 26–30
Kennedy's actions in, 26–30
McCarthyism and, 25
college students, deferments of,
71, 72, 117
combat techniques, U.S.,
55–56, 60
combat troops, U.S., 55, 57–59
discipline problems among,
72, 116–18
Vietnamese as viewed by, 59,
65–67
Communism
in Cold War period, 21–30
Domino Theory and, 20, 136
as patriotic fervor, 69

see also Ho Chi Minh;
National Liberation
Front; North Vietnam
Congress, U.S., 3, 135
antiwar sentiments in, 76,
115, 118, 123, 128, 131
Gulf of Tonkin events and,
33, 35–36, 118
Con Thien, 79, 80
credibility gap, 95–96
C. Turner Joy (destroyer), 34–35
Cuban crisis, 26–28
Culverhouse, Jerry R., 106

Dak To, 79
Da Lat, 91, 93
Da Nang, 39–40, 91
dap loi (booby traps), 58
Davis, James Thomas, 32
de Castries, Christian, 10–14
de Galard-Terraube,
Geneviève, 13, 14
Democratic Republic of
Vietnam (DRV), see North
Vietnam
desertions, military, 72, 126
Diem, Ngo Dinh, 17, 28, 65
Kennedy's support of, 29
opposition to, 18–20, 29–30
Dien Bien Phu, battle of, 1,
8–15, 50, 96
DMZ (Demilitarized Zone), 16,
63
combat near, 59, 78, 79, 120
"Doves," 69–71, 96
draft evaders, 72, 126
draft issues, 70, 71–72, 117,
126
Drug Abuse Task Force, 118
Dulles, John Foster, 3

economy, U.S., effect of
Vietnam War on, 37, 76,
99, 111

Eisenhower, Dwight D., 1–3, 7, 17, 20, 67–68
election of 1968, 76, 95, 96, 99–100
election of 1972, 121–22, 129
Ellsberg, Daniel, 98–99, 129
Ely, Paul, 1–3, 13

Fall, Bernard, 15
Feiffer, Jules, 71
F-80 Shooting Stars, 52
First Cavalry Airmobile Division, U.S., 40, 59–60
FitzGerald, Frances, 77
Fonda, Jane, 71
Ford, Gerald R., 128, 130
fragging of officers, 117
Free Fire Zones, 55, 56, 62, 65, 77
French Foreign Legion, 11
French Indochina War, 1–15, 50, 60
  U.S. support for, 1–2, 3, 7
"frogmen," U.S. Navy, 33

Geneva Peace Conference, 14, 16–17
Germany, division of, 23, 27
Giap, Vo Nguyen, 5–6, 8–12, 18, 49, 90, 113, 114
Goldwater, Barry, 36, 37
Grauwin, Paul, 13
Great Britain, 21, 23, 25
Great Society program, 37, 76, 99
Green Berets, see Special Forces
Gruening, Ernest, 36
"grunts," 55
guerrilla warfare, 5, 6, 8, 32, 49–59, 73, 114
  in French Indochina War, 5–6, 8, 49
  tunnels used in, 66

U.S. unpreparedness for, 56–58
Gulf of Tonkin Resolution (1964), 35–36, 98, 118

Haiphong, bombings of, 5, 51, 120–21, 122–23
Halberstam, David, 34–35, 97
Hamburger Hill action, 112
Hanoi, bombings of, 51–52, 120, 122–23
"Hawks," 69, 70, 72, 96, 136
helicopters, 53–54, 60
Henderson, Oran K., 106
Heng Samrin, 132
herbicides, 77
heroin, 118
Herrick, John, 34
Hershey, Lewis, 72
Ho Chi Minh, 4, 7, 15, 17, 24, 39, 89–90, 112
Ho Chi Minh Trail, 33, 39, 62, 79, 118, 119
"hot pursuit" principle, 61
Hue, 91, 94, 108
  destruction of, 67, 94
Humphrey, Hubert, 101

Ia Drang Valley battle, 59–61
intelligence activities, 19, 26–27
  by U.S., in Vietnam, 28, 30, 60, 78, 79, 98
international relief agencies, 133
Iron Triangle attack, 75, 77

Japan, 3–4
Johnson, Lyndon B., 20, 28, 30, 39, 76, 115, 126
  antiwar criticism and, 70, 74, 76, 96–97
  Great Society and, 37, 76, 99
  1968 election decision of, 99–100

1968 Tet offensive and, 79–80, 95–96
reelection of (1964), 36
secret warfare under, 33, 39, 98
Tonkin Gulf events and, 35–36, 98
Joint Chiefs of Staff, U.S., 2, 38, 79, 80, 115, 119
"Jolly Green Giants," 53
journalists, 92–93, 94
war criticism and, 74, 75, 76, 80, 118
jungle defoliation, 50–51, 77, 79

Kennedy, John F., 20, 37
Cold War crises of, 26–30
Vietnam policies of, 28–30, 32
Kennedy, Robert F., 33, 100
Kent State University, 116
Khanh, Nguyen, 31
Khe Sanh, 79, 80, 91
as U.S. Dien Bien Phu, 93–94
Khmer Rouge, 131–33
Khrushchev, Nikita, 27–28
kill ratios, 79, 95
Kissinger, Henry, 113, 115, 118, 120–23, 125, 130–31
Korean War, 3, 7, 16, 24–26, 52, 72
Koster, Samuel, 106, 107
Ky, Nguyen Cao, 31–32, 74

Lam Son Operation, 118–19
Langlais, Pierre, 10–14
Laos, 3, 4, 8, 9, 17, 33, 78, 112
bombings of, 33, 39, 113, 119, 127
invasion of, 118–19, 136
Le Duc Tho, 113, 121, 122, 130

LeMay, Curtis, 113
Lodge, Henry Cabot, 113
Loeschner, Bobbie, 109–10
Lon Nol, 115, 128, 131

McCarthy, Eugene, 95, 99–100
McCarthy, Joseph R., 25
McGovern, George, 121–22, 129
McNamara, Robert, 38, 62, 63, 95, 96–98
Maddox (destroyer), 34–35
Manchester, William, 122–23
Mao Tse-tung, 5–6, 24
marijuana, 118
Marines, U.S., 39–40, 54–55, 91, 93–94, 128
Marshall Plan, 22–23
Medina, Ernest, 104
Mekong Delta region, 78, 91, 114
MiG interceptor aircraft, 52
military advisors, 17, 20, 29, 32, 33, 38
Miller, David J., 70
Millians, Daniel R., 106
Mitchell, John, 98
M-1 rifles, 57
Montagnards, 32, 59–60
Monte Cassino monastery, 68
Morrison, Norman, 70, 97
Morse, Wayne, 36
My Lai massacre, 67, 103–8, 112

napalm, 51
National Liberation Front (NLF), 68–69, 113
NATO, 24
Navarre, Henri, 3, 8–10, 12–13
Navy, U.S., 33–35, 39, 62
New York Times, 98, 99
Nguyen Van Troi, 97
Nhu, Ngo Dinh, 19, 29, 30

Nixon, Richard M., 20, 61, 71, 98, 101, 127
My Lai massacre and, 103–4, 107
war policy of, 102, 103, 111–15, 118–24, 125
Watergate Affair and, 128–30
Nobel Peace Prize, 130
North Vietnam (Democratic Republic of Vietnam; DRV)
in French Indochina War, 1–15
Geneva Agreements and, 16–17
Ho's changes in, 17–18
South Vietnam overrun by, 128
Tonkin Gulf events and, 34–35
see also Ho Chi Minh; Vietcong; Vietminh
North Vietnamese Army (AVN), 18, 59–61, 78, 91, 113, 127

Operation Cedar Falls, 75, 77
Operation Complete Victory, 100
Operation Junction City, 75, 77
Operation Pegasus, 94
Operation Rolling Thunder, 39, 49–50, 51
Operation Starlite, 55

pacification programs, 63–66
"Peace with Honor" goal, 113, 125
Peers, William R., 108
Pentagon Papers, 98–99, 119, 129
Pham Van Dong, 112, 122, 123
Pleiku, 59–60
Pol Pot, 131, 133

Porter, William J., 120
prisoner-of-war issue, 122, 124
punji pits (booby traps), 58

racism issues, 67, 117
refugees, 65, 77, 79, 95, 114, 126, 131, 132–33
resources control program, 79
rice crop, destruction of, 79
Ridenhour, Ronald L., 103–4, 107
Ridgway, Matthew B., 3
Roosevelt, Franklin D., 21, 76–77
Rusk, Dean, 38, 97

Saigon, 38, 77, 128
religious riots in, 29–30
in Tet offensive, 91–93
SAMs (missiles), 52–53
Search and Destroy actions, 55, 62
SEATO, 26, 35
secrecy, covert operations, 78
Pentagon Papers and, 98–99, 119, 129
on U.S. involvement, 33, 39, 40, 113, 115, 127
self-determination principle, 4
Shrike (antiradar missile), 53
Sihanouk, Norodom, 115
South Vietnam (Republic of South Vietnam)
ancestral land in, 64, 65
election issue in, 16, 17, 18, 64–65
environmental destruction of, 50–51, 67, 77, 79, 94
in French Indochina War, 1–15
Geneva Agreements and, 16–17
North Vietnam takeover of (1975), 128, 131

political instability of, 19–20, 38, 74

U.S. military support of, 17, 20, 29, 31, 33, 38–40, 55, 60, 62, 73–74, 76, 96–97, 100, 111, 126, 127

see also ARVN; Diem, Ngo Dinh; Thieu, Nguyen Van

South Vietnamese militia, 73

Soviet Union, 3, 115, 121, 123
Cold War and, 21–24
North Vietnam aided by, 51–52, 57

Spanish-American War, 57

Special Forces (Green Berets), 32–33, 56, 59–60, 65–66

Spock, Benjamin, 71

spy trials, in U.S., 24

Stalin, Joseph, 21–23, 26

Strategic Hamlet program, 64, 65

student antiwar demonstrations, 70, 72, 115–16

Taiwan (Formosa), 6, 24

Taylor, Maxwell, 28, 38

technology, U.S. military's reliance on, 49–54, 57, 63

Tet, described, 89

Tet offensive (1968), 89–96, 100
casualties in, 94–95, 114
"funeral" deception in, 90–91
preparations for, 79–80
truce agreement and, 89–90
U.S. public misled on, 95–96

Thailand, 38, 53, 62, 131, 132–33

Thieu, Nguyen Van, 31, 74, 113, 121, 122, 128, 131

Thompson, Hugh C., Jr., 105–6, 108

Truman, Harry S, 2–3, 7, 20, 22

Truman Doctrine, 22

United Nations, 22

veterans, Vietnam, 133–35

"Victor Charlies," 57

Vietcong (National Liberation Front of South Vietnam), 18–19, 30, 38
casualties, 77, 79, 119, 127
in 1968 Tet offensive, 79–80, 89–96, 114
in 1972 spring offensive, 120–21
political activities of, *see* National Liberation Front
South Vietnam infiltrated by, 50–51, 56, 63, 64–66, 111, 114
strength in South Vietnam of, 31, 50, 63, 65–66, 73, 78
supplies for, 50, 51–52, 57, 120
see also guerrilla warfare

Vietminh, 4–7, 8–9, 16, 17, 18, 24

Vietnam, *see* French Indochina War; North Vietnam; South Vietnam

Vietnamese children, adoption of, 109–10

Vietnamese National Army, 8

Vietnamese shrines and cultural centers, destruction of, 67–68, 94

Vietnamization, 102, 111, 112, 113, 114, 118, 119

Tet-offensive interpretation
and, 114
Vietnam Veterans of America,
135
Vietnam War
aftermath of, 125–37
air war in, *see* aerial warfare
care and concern for civilians
by U.S. personnel in,
108–10
civilian casualties in, 59, 62,
78, 94–95, 103–8, 121,
126, 127
Cold War and, 21–30
conventional vs. unconventional warfare in, *see*
guerrilla warfare
cost of, 125–27
Geneva Agreements and,
16–17
hardliners' postwar view of,
136
"McNamara's Line" in, 63
major ground combats in,
54–55, 59–61, 75, 78,
89–96, 120–21
opposition in U.S. to, *see*
antiwar criticism
"Ouch Theory" of, 39
peace talks in, 39, 101,
112–13, 120, 121–22,
123
"Peace with Honor" goal in,
113, 125
as political vs. military
conflict, 63–64

secrecy on, 33, 39, 40, 78,
98–99, 113, 115, 119,
127, 129
U.S. and Allied casualties in,
32, 53, 72, 95, 100, 111,
112, 121, 125–27
U.S. commitment to, 15, 38,
40
U.S. domestic issues and, 37,
76, 99, 101, 111,
121–22, 129
U.S. ground troops
withdrawn from, 111,
112, 113, 114, 118, 120,
123–24
U.S. public's postwar
reactions 133–37
U.S. State Department and,
61

Walt, Lewis, 55
Washington, D.C., antiwar
protest (November 1969),
71
Watergate Affair, 128–30
Westmoreland, William, 38, 55,
56, 59, 62, 73, 77, 78, 100
1968 Tet offensive and,
79–80, 91, 93, 95–96
U.S. public relations tours
of, 74–76, 77
Weyland, Frederick, 119
World War II, 3–4, 49, 50, 56,
67–68, 76

Zippo Brigades, 65

AUTHOR BIOGRAPHY

DON LAWSON is the author of over twenty books on war history, including the eleven volumes in his Young People's History of America's Wars series. He believes that to achieve peace we must first understand war and therefore writes mainly on military subjects.

Don Lawson attended Cornell College, Iowa, and the University of Iowa Writers' Workshop. He edited a weekly newspaper in Nora Springs, Iowa, and spent four years in the U.S. Army Air Force. He is now Editor in Chief of United Educators, Inc. His most recent book for Crowell, *FDR's New Deal,* was an American Library Association Notable Book for 1979.